Nationalism

Also available in Papermac

Collected Poems and Plays
Glimpses of Bengal
My Reminiscences
Selected Short Stories

Nationalism

Rabindranath Tagore

M

PAPERMAC

First published by Macmillan & Co. 1917

This edition published in paperback 1991 by
PAPERMAC
a division of Macmillan Publishers Limited
Cavaye Place London SW10 9PG
and Basingstoke

Associated companies in Auckland, Delhi, Dublin, Gaborone,
Hamburg, Harare, Hong Kong, Johannesburg, Kuala Lumpur,
Lagos, Manzini, Melbourne, Mexico City, Nairobi, New York,
Singapore and Tokyo

ISBN 0-333-54581-8

A CIP catalogue record for this book is available from the
British Library

Printed in Hong Kong

Contents

Introduction

The lectures on which *Nationalism* is based were delivered not in India but in Japan and the United States. C. F. Andrews, who accompanied Rabindranath Tagore on his Japanese tour, says that the first two chapters were written for lectures in Japan and 'at white heat'. (The lecture on 'Nationalism in India' appears – although only once – among his lectures in America.) The Japanese tour occupied Tagore from late May until early September 1916, then he revised the same lectures and crossed and re-crossed the United States lecturing from September 1916 until January 1917. Undoubtedly the theme of nationalism was obsessing the poet at that time. To the disappointment of some of his American audiences, who had hoped for more poetic readings and discourses, he confined himself almost exclusively to this topic, speaking on 'Nationalism' and 'The Cult of Nationalism' more than twenty times, as he tracked from the West Coast via Salt Lake City, Denver, Milwaukee, Nashville, Cincinnati, Detroit, to the major East Coast cities and back again to the West.

The poet was then aged 55. He had been thrown

somewhat suddenly on to a world stage by the enthusiastic acclaim in English literary circles for his own free translations from Bengali of his *Gitanjali* songs, widely perceived as representing the wisdom and poetic mysticism of 'the East' – followed by the award (in 1913) of the Nobel prize for literature: he was the first Asian writer to become a Nobel laureate. A knighthood succeeded. The poet, with his noble and beautiful presence, his beard and flowing robes, bearing the mystery of an impenetrable alien culture, seemed to come forward to meet an already existing need in the West – a West that had little means of judging the merits of Tagore's poetry from the inadequacy of the available translations – for who in the literary West knew Bengali? If it were not for the fact that Tagore was indeed a major literary and intellectual figure, the whole episode could be caricatured as a classic case of 'Western Orientalism'.

Tagore found his emergence into the searchlight of world reputation to be profoundly disturbing. He was already known for his swift alternation between phases of activist commitment to several causes and retirement into meditation and writing, either at the school which he had founded at his father's ashram Shantiniketan ('Abode of Peace') in rural West Bengal, or on his *zamindari* at Shelidah, a family estate on the banks of the Padma in East Bengal (now Bangladesh). Yet after each phase of retirement he was drawn back into highly public activity like a moth to flame. When he received the Nobel award one of his first laments was that he would never again have any peace. In January 1914, he wrote to my father: 'Since I have got my European reputation the world is too much with me. . . . It simply chokes me and offers me not a morsel of food.' And in the previous December: 'It is a great trial I am undergoing. This sudden outburst of applause acts upon me like a dust storm that blinds and bewilders and brings no cooling rain.'

Yet he was attracted back again and again to these very visible and exacting public appearances, with their packed auditoriums and receptions. Undoubtedly in one part of himself he was exhilarated and saw this as his 'destiny' or prophetic 'mission'. When my father was writing his two studies of Tagore,* he was given the most expert and unstinting advice and criticism by a young scholar at Calcutta University, Prasanta Mahalanobis. (Though a physicist by training and subsequently India's leading statistician, Mahalanobis had an unrivalled knowledge of Tagore's life and work, and a better command of his early literary canon than the poet himself could recall.) In a letter of October 1920 he commented on Tagore's 'dual personality':

He loves solitude but cannot live in it for any length of time. There is something in him which goads him on to a mad incessant whirlpool of activity. This lasts for some time – then he gives up everything in a single night and again retires into solitude. . . . After the intense propaganda work of Swadeshi** he resigned his membership of every Committee, severed the connection with every organisation – all in the course of a single day and fled to [Shantiniketan] from where he could not be dragged out for several years.

That was in 1907, and the next years were productive in poetry and plays. In 1910–11 he suddenly emerged

* E. J. Thompson, *Rabindranath Tagore: his Life and Work*, Calcutta, 1921 and *Rabindranath Tagore: Poet and Dramatist*, Oxford, 1926; revised edn 1948.

** Literally 'our country', the name given to the patriotic movement mounted against the 1905 Partition of Bengal.

3

again in Calcutta, to take an active part in the reform movement in his 'church', the Brahmo Samaj. Baulked by the conservative faction, he retired for a year or more to Shantiniketan – 'then all on a sudden his *Gitanjali* tour of England and America'. Then retreat to Shantiniketan once more (where he received the news of his Nobel prize in November 1913), until the restlessness was aroused again. In April 1916 he wrote to my father, with a poet's licence of unpracticality, that he was going 'to the south, and then – I know not where, possibly across the Pacific.' His guess was quite right. He was off on the 'Nationalism' tour, via Japan to the United States. The American tour was abruptly cut short by nervous exhaustion before all engagements had been fulfilled.

One ostensible motive for these lecture-tours was to raise funds for his school (and, later, university) at Shantiniketan. But Tagore was subject to other pressures which we must understand. Tagore the poet was becoming overwhelmed by Tagore the international public man – an embodiment in the world's eyes of Indian culture and (perhaps) national identity. Increasingly Tagore was ceasing to be a free agent and was captive to his own reputation, which assigned to him a public role from which he could not escape. Nor, despite his private complaints, did he try very hard to escape. His tours of Europe and America were themselves a figurement of his constant themes, the meeting of East and West, and the search for World Culture and Universal Man. He was fulfilling his 'destiny'. As he wrote to C. F. Andrews in July 1920, from London: 'When I am in the West . . . I am in touch with those who feel and express their need of me.' He felt 'a constant surprise' that 'these enormously busy people have listened to a voice from the distant East.' 'I am received in a living world of mind.' And in a letter from France shortly afterwards, he was feeling homesick for the ashram at Shantiniketan: 'But at the same time I know that unless my relationship with the wide world of humanity grows in truth and love, my relationship with the Ashram will not be perfect.'

There were historical pressures also behind *Nationalism*. Most evident is the impact of the first world war. The pre-war decade had seen the high tide of a rhetoric of benevolent liberalism and a universalism which offered to comprehend the great achievements of the cultures of both West and East. Tagore himself was deeply influenced by this moment, as were such leading contemporary Bengali intellectuals as the philosopher Brajendranath Seal, a close ally and interpreter of Tagore, whose eloquent and polymathic *New Essays in Criticism* (1903) is a neo-Hegelian essay on the theme, so germane to Tagore, of universal humanity:

> The divers historic cultures, arts, religions, phil-osophemes, codes, race-consciousness, are not partial phases or aspects of Humanity, or of the Absolute Ideal; they are the developing whole, and express, more or less fully, more or less accurately, the Idea of Universal Humanity.

The gates of entry to this universal republic were the arts or philosophy, and the only fee fair-mindedness. Tagore had been nurtured in the rhetoric of the universal republic of letters, and he never repudiated these formative influences. In his remarkable 1941 address on his eightieth birthday he recalled that 'it was mainly through their mighty literature that we formed our ideas' of the British. In his childhood 'discussions centred upon Shakespeare's drama and Byron's poetry and above all, upon the large-hearted

5

liberalism of 19th century English politics'. 'What was remarkable . . . was the way in which we gave our recognition to human greatness even when it revealed itself in the foreigner.' For the Indian commercial and patrician élites, to which Tagore belonged, the rhetoric of the pre-war years was that of the Indianisation of administration, the law, and education: Indian graduates from Oxbridge were diluting the British hegemony; honours and titles were being awarded in the benign climate of Lord Hardinge's Viceroyalty. Tagore's warm acclaim in England in 1912, the Nobel award and the knighthood which followed were all part of that climate of liberalism. Tagore's own rejection of extremism was seen, in British eyes, as an appropriate and matching response.

The world war made a mockery of this enlightened rhetoric. On the outbreak of war, Brajendranath Seal wrote to my father:

Oh . . . this insane crime against civilisation! What becomes of the militarist plea that the best guarantee of peace is this preparedness for war? No, these weapons are forged to be used; and the preparations inevitably end in that which is their professed end.

And a few days later he fulminated against the 'feather-brained bipeds on our dunghill of an Earth':

However you *spell* it, war *means* murder, robbery, rape, arson, and all the other felonies compounded in one explosive ingredient, and of all crimes, nationalism today is perhaps the blackest and deadliest when, animated by the earth-grabbing propensity, it pursues its object in a way necessarily leading to war. . . .

6

The poisoning of the water supply; the indiscriminate scattering of mines, in an open sea along the traffic route; the dropping of bombs from the air on inoffensive populations – are being freely resorted to, today, in the name of patriotism and nationalism, by the proud inheritors of a soi-disant civilisation.

In 1919, when my father returned to India from the war he wrote: 'The War has shocked India unspeakably, has seemed a collapse. It is felt by very many that Christianity is discredited so utterly that it is no longer a matter for argument.' To Tagore the war 'was nothing but a volcano shattering itself with fearful convulsions, the robber-civilisation of Europe flaming to well-deserved ruin'. One of Tagore's strongest expressions of this comes not in *Nationalism* but in *Creative Unity* (1922), after he had visited the battlefields of France:

The awful calm of desolation, which still bore wrinkles of pain – death-struggles stiffened into ugly ridges – brought before my mind the vision of a huge demon, which had no shape, no meaning, yet had two arms that could strike and break and tear, a gaping mouth that could devour, and bulging brains that could conspire and plan.

This passage is singled out for comment in the major study of Tagore by my father, who rebuked Tagore for having 'an inadequate conception of what we had suffered. . . . No man should let himself be at the mercy of his similes, especially when speaking of recent sorrow.'

*

The world war is not a central theme of *Nationalism*. It is, rather, ever present in the background, as proof of the self-destructive tendency of the organised modern nation. It provides an apocalyptic ground base to the whole argument: 'This European war of Nations is the war of retribution', 'the veil has been raised, and in this frightful war the West has stood face to face with her own creation, to which she had offered her soul.' The world war was the fulfilment of the necessary logic of aggressive western materialism, of science divorced from spirituality, by which the Nation will drag the greater part of the world 'down into the bottom of destruction. Whenever Power removes all checks from its path . . . it triumphantly rides into its ultimate crash of death.'

It would be folly to accuse Tagore of sentimental alarmism. *Nationalism* is a prescient, even prophetic, work whose foresight has been confirmed by sufficient evidence – two world wars, the nuclear arms race, environmental disasters, technologies too clever to be controlled. If its assertive denunciations of the Nation sometimes appear to be repetitious and tedious, this is in part because the indictment has become over-familiar since Tagore drew it up. Yet it must be confessed that the lectures succeed better as prophecy than diagnosis. Tagore enforces his message by assertion and by colourful metaphors rather than by analysis. His conclusions are assumed to be true in proportion to the vehemence with which they are asserted.

As should be expected, the connotations of the term 'nationalism' have changed a good deal since 1916. Tagore has little to say about ethnic cultures, or about linguistic or religious communities or nationalist myths. His definition of a nation is the political and economic union of a people 'in that aspect which a whole population assumes when organised for a mechanical purpose'. The emphasis falls upon *organised* and *mechanical*. The western Nation is conterminous with the nation-state, the mechanical organisation of peoples in pursuit of material aggrandisement and hence necessarily aggressive and imperialist in character; in fact, for 'nationalism' we might often read 'imperialism'. At other times, Tagore, in his distrust of technology and impersonal bureaucracy, falls into positions akin to the western Romantic critique of 'civilisation' and 'modernisation': 'This abstract being, the Nation, is ruling India,' and he is able to take the British rule as exemplar of an impersonal and mechanical organisation, 'which is as little touched by the human hand as possible'.

But Tagore rarely enters an indictment, however severe, without also entering a qualification. His thought continually moves between opposites – spiritual and materialist, East and West, Nation and no-nation, masculine and feminine, abstract and personal – and then seeks for ways to reconcile and 'harmonise' the opposites. Thus, the West also has a great spiritual inheritance, East and West should complement each other, so also should Woman and Man, and Reason and Spirit (or science and poetry) need not compete but should harmonise. In *Nationalism* this is rarely more than wishful rhetoric, but there is a more arduous pursuit of this dialectic in his poetry and in other writings. To the Nation he opposed 'The World of Personality' – all social relations that were not mechanical and impersonal. (He lectured several times in the United States on this theme, and his collection *Personality* (1917) was published on the heels of *Nationalism*.) Here Tagore wrestled with themes of contradiction and its transcendence, and he sought to combine for his American audiences the wisdom of the ancient *Isha Upanishad* with that of Walt Whitman, both of which expound the ways in which the infinite must always find expression in finite form and in finite space and time:

> There is a point where in the mystery of existence contradictions meet; where movement is not all movement and stillness is not all stillness; where the idea and the form, the within and the without, are united; where infinite becomes finite, yet not losing its infinity.

Yet the contradiction between nationalism and no-nationhood did not admit of such a verbal reconciliation, and this contradiction limited the success of Tagore's lectures on nationalism. It can be seen that Tagore commenced these in Japan by offering his respects not only to the Japanese cultural inheritance but also to the supposed presence of pan-Asian spiritual values which contrasted with the aggressive materialism of the western Nation. But his conviction soon faltered, as he observed exactly the same features of material greed, mechanical organisation and imperialist aggression in modernising Japan: 'What is dangerous for Japan is, not the imitation of the outward features of the West, but the acceptance of the motive force of western nationalism as her own.'

Tagore's outspoken criticisms did not please Japanese audiences and the welcome given to him on first arrival soon cooled. He for his part held himself somewhat aloof, mixed little with Japanese intellectuals, and gave few lectures. He concluded that his Japanese visit had been a failure. Japanese critics suggested that Tagore's praise for the lack of nationalism in Indian history was the special pleading of a 'defeated people'. In the United States he was received with more enthusiasm: there were Tagore 'cultists' in some cities, and also an energetic lecture-tour promoter. America had not yet entered the European war, and Tagore was careful to suggest that, as a young multiracial nation, the USA did not merit the full commination visited upon the rest of the West. Indeed, Tagore suggested a parallel between India and America, insofar as both served as willing hosts to diverse immigrations. But Tagore's American audiences could not fail to recognise their own features in his diatribes against materialism, technology, mechanical organisation, and the unbridled pursuit of wealth, and some resented being scolded 'at $700 a scold'.

It is Tagore's relations with his own people – and with Indian nationalism – which present the most complex problem. In the period after the war it was generally supposed that Tagore had himself passed through an ardent nationalistic phase in the first years of the century – the years of Swadeshi and of the agitation against the 1905 partition of Bengal – and that he then fell back into a more quietist stance in the next decade. His novel *The Home and the World* (1916 in Bengali) belongs to this latter phase, and it testifies to the ambivalence of Tagore's response to Indian nationalism. Nationalists accused him of apostasy, which seemed to be confirmed when he was awarded a knighthood in 1915. (His renunciation of that honour in 1919, in protest at the massacre at Amritsar and its aftermath, did something to repair his patriotic image.) Yet at the same time Tagore's lack of partisanship, his employment of an aloof sarcasm in the face of the rituals of the British Raj, his fair-mindedness which put him above British administrators and Indian patriots alike, were sometimes a more effective criticism of power than overblown nationalist rhetoric.

When my father published his first short book on Tagore (in 1921) he accepted the generally held view – that Tagore had once been a nationalist, but had now withdrawn from this stance. Prasanta Mahalanobis, who had given such generous help in the preparation of the book, was deeply critical of these judgements and urged my father to rewrite these passages. He told him that he had misunderstood Tagore almost completely on the question of nationalism: 'He never supported nationalism, not in any form or guise.' 'Even at the height of the Swadeshi movement he was protesting against some particular aspects of the movement' (December 1921). And there is a long letter from Mahalanobis of about the same date which discussed the whole question. This clarifies the issues in so many ways that it deserves presenting fully:

[Tagore] believes in serving one's country in constructive work. Hence his emphasis on village work, mass education, sanitation and social reform. He believes in India – in future possibilities as well as in her great past – but does not believe in nationalism. The greatness of India consists in her recognition of *human* values – in her message of *social civilisation*. R[abindranath] believes that the only permanent solution of world-problems – of international conflicts – depends on the proper recognition of this fact – that *socialisation* is the only way out. R. has always insisted that this has been the message of India throughout her past history. He does not believe in political freedom as an end in itself. 'Swaraj' or political freedom is desirable for two things – first it will accelerate a more intimate socialisation – a more organised unification of India and hence secondly contribute to the saving of Europe. . . . He himself has never professed to take any interest in politics. He believes Congress [Party] work to be useful only in as much as it tends to bring the different peoples of India into closer contact – that is, in the socialising effects of politics.

Mahalanobis continued: 'He does not believe in asking for boons from the British Government – simply because he does not care much for political boons.' Instead, 'We must awaken our own deep-seated springs of action for good.' Tagore advocated neither the boycott of government institutions nor co-operation with them – 'not to seek favour, nor to depend on Govt. for education, sanitation, nor even for peace and order or justice. . . . He does not want to give any importance to Govt. action.'

He wants our mind to be completely *free* of Govt. influence. This is why he has always placed moderatism and extremism or cooperation and non-cooperation in the same category. Both are obsessed with their thoughts of Govt. Both aim at bringing pressure to bear upon Govt. Both want political concessions. Their methods differ but their fundamental attitude is the same.

As for the contrary evidence of Tagore's 'patriotic' gestures, such as his renunciation of his knighthood, 'R. believes in protesting against injustice in the name of humanity, not in the hope of gaining concessions, not as a political weapon, not for creating race-feeling, but simply because it is a fundamental moral duty.' One may accept this, while not accepting the implication that Tagore was the only one whose protests were motivated by a sense of moral duty.

Mahalanobis's remarkable letter states some matters more explicitly and fully than Tagore (with his infuriating evasion of the specific) did himself in *Nationalism*, although there are many passages in the lectures which confirm Prasanta Mahalanobis's analysis. Despite pleas from Gandhi, Tagore refused his consent to negative or destructive actions – the boycott, the burning of foreign cloth, and the obsession with spinning (the *charka*). He was to withhold his support, in the early 1920s, from non-cooperation in colleges and schools: as he wrote to Andrews in March 1921, the students were committed 'not to fuller education but to non-education'. Above all, he summoned his fellow-countrymen to set about reforming and renewing their own society – agricultural improvement, social welfare, education, the overcoming of barriers erected by caste and religion – by their own efforts and not be begging alms from their foreign rulers. Power should not be matched by the organisation of anti-power, but should be ignored. Tagore was a founder of 'anti-politics'.

There are difficulties in this refusal, although both Gandhi and Nehru respected Tagore's position, consulted him, and regarded him as the 'conscience' of India. But we need to reflect upon the strengths of the position also. For Tagore, more than any other thinker of his time, had a clear conception of civil society, as something distinct from and of stronger and more personal texture than political or economic structures. In his view, despite successive invasions and conquests, civil society in India had survived as an organic reality. India 'remained aloof' from the fights and intrigues of her rulers and conquerors,

> Because her homes, her fields, her temples of worship, her schools, where her teachers and students lived together in the atmosphere of simplicity and devotion and learning, her village self-government with its simple laws and peaceful administration – all these truly belonged to her. But her thrones were not her concern.

This idealised picture of Indian history was suited to Tagore's conclusion: 'Society as such has no ulterior purpose. It is an end in itself. It is a spontaneous self-expression of man as a social being.' One of the gravest offences of the cult of the Nation was that it forced individuals to surrender their personal wills into an abstract organised National will, and to give their loyalty to its impersonal goals.

I have tried to rub some of the quaintness off the expression of Tagore's ideas in English in *Nationalism* and to show that they hold together well and also match the actions of his life. So far from being out-moded, Tagore's commitment to anti-politics and his concern with civil society make him appear at times to be a markedly modern – or perhaps post-modern? – thinker. So also with his courageous espousal of the values of universalism in the face of nationalist taunts. As the old universalisms – pre-1914 liberalism, Marxism and the claims of the Third International – have collapsed or been devalued, so these values are in need of rediscovery in a new form today. The assertive nationalisms and communalisms which mark our own time and which refuse any assent to universal values are not confined to the West. India herself is no longer a people of no-nation, nor a people united in nationalist opposition to British rule, but a subcontinent containing competing nationalist sensitivities. Tagore cannot resolve these problems, but if we can share and apply his far-sighted intuitions he may help us do so.

E. P. Thompson

Nationalism in Japan

I

The worst form of bondage is the bondage of dejection, which keeps men hopelessly chained in loss of faith in themselves. We have been repeatedly told, with some justification, that Asia lives in the past – it is like a rich mausoleum which displays all its magnificence in trying to immortalise the dead. It was said of Asia that it could never move in the path of progress, its face was so inevitably turned backwards. We accepted this accusation, and came believe it. In India, I know, a large section of our educated community, grown tired of feeling the humiliation of this charge against us, is trying with all its resources of self-deception to turn it into a matter of boasting. But boasting is only a masked shame, it does not truly believe in itself.

When things stood still like this, and we in Asia hypnotised ourselves into the belief that it could never by any possibility be otherwise, Japan rose from her dreams, and in giant strides left centuries of inaction behind, overtaking the present time in its foremost achievement. This has broken the spell under which we lay in torpor for ages, taking it to be the normal condition of certain races living in certain geographical limits. We forgot that in Asia great kingdoms were founded, philosophy, science, arts and literatures flourished, and all the great religions of the world had their cradles. Therefore it cannot be said that there is anything inherent in the soil and climate of Asia to produce mental inactivity and to atrophy the faculties which impel men to go forward. For centuries we did hold torches of civilisation in the East when the West slumbered in darkness, and that could never be the sign of sluggish minds or narrowness of vision.

Then fell the darkness of night upon all the lands of the East. The current of time seemed to stop at once, and Asia ceased to take any new food, feeding upon its own past, which is really feeding upon itself. The stillness seemed like death, and the great voice was silenced which sent forth messages of eternal truth that have saved man's life from pollution for generations, like the ocean of air that keeps the earth sweet, ever cleansing its impurities.

But life has its sleep, its periods of inactivity, when it loses its movements, takes no new food, living upon its past storage. Then it grows helpless, its muscles relaxed, and it easily lends itself to be jeered at for its stupor. In the rhythm of life, pauses there must be for the renewal of life. Life in its activity is ever spending itself, burning all its fuel. This extravagance cannot go on indefinitely, but is always followed by a passive stage, when all expenditure is stopped and all adventures abandoned in favour of rest and slow recuperation.

The tendency of mind is economical; it loves to form habits and move in grooves which save it the trouble of thinking anew at each of its steps. Ideals once formed make the mind lazy. It becomes afraid to risk its acquisitions in fresh endeavours. It tries to enjoy complete security by shutting up its belongings behind fortifications of habits. But this is really shutting oneself up from the fullest enjoyment of one's own possessions. It is miserliness. The living ideals must not lose their touch with the growing and changing life. Their real freedom is not within the boundaries of security, but on the high-road of adventures, full of the risk of new experiences.

One morning the whole world looked up in surprise when Japan broke through her walls of old habits in a night and came out triumphant. It was done in such an incredibly short time that it seemed like a change of dress and not like the building up of a new structure. She showed the confident strength of maturity, and the freshness and infinite potentiality of new life at the same moment. The fear was entertained that it was a mere freak of history, a child's game of Time, the blowing up of a soap-bubble, perfect in its rondure and colouring, hollow in its heart and without substance. But Japan has proved conclusively that this sudden revealment of her power is not a short-lived wonder, a chance product of time and tide, thrown up from the depth of obscurity to be swept away the next moment into a sea of oblivion.

The truth is that Japan is old and new at the same time. She has her legacy of ancient culture from the East – the culture that enjoins man to look for his true wealth and power in his inner soul, the culture that gives self-possession in the face of loss and danger, self-sacrifice without counting the cost or hoping for gain, defiance of death, acceptance of countless social obligations that we owe to men as social beings. In a word, modern Japan has come out of the immemorial East like a lotus blossoming in easy grace, all the while keeping its firm hold upon the profound depth from which it has sprung.

And Japan, the child of the Ancient East, has also fearlessly claimed all the gifts of the modern age for herself. She has shown her bold spirit in breaking through the confinements of habits, useless accumulations of the lazy mind, which seeks safety in its thrift and its locks and keys. Thus she has come in contact with the living time and has accepted with eagerness and aptitude the responsibilities of modern civilisation.

This it is which has given heart to the rest of Asia. We have seen that the life and the strength are there in us; only the dead crust has to be removed. We have seen that taking shelter in the dead is death itself, and only taking all the risk of life to the fullest extent is living.

I, for myself, cannot believe that Japan has become what she is by imitating the West. We cannot imitate life, we cannot simulate strength for long, nay, what is more, a mere imitation is a source of weakness. For it hampers our true nature; it is always in our way. It is like dressing our skeleton with another man's skin, giving rise to eternal feuds between the skin and the bones at every movement.

The real truth is that science is not man's nature, it is mere knowledge and training. By knowing the laws of the material universe you do not change your deeper humanity. You can borrow knowledge from others, but you cannot borrow temperament.

But at the imitative stage of our schooling we cannot distinguish between the essential and the non-essential, between what is transferable and what is not. It is something like the faith of the primitive mind in the magical properties of the accidents of outward forms which accompany some real truth. We are afraid of leaving out something valuable and efficacious by not swallowing the husk with the kernel. But while our greed delights in wholesale appropriation, it is the function of our vital nature to assimilate, which is the only true appropriation for a living organism. Where there is life it is sure to assert itself by its choice of acceptance and refusal according to its constitutional necessity. The living organism does not allow itself to grow into its food; it changes its food into its own body. And only thus can it grow strong and not by mere accumulation, or by giving up its personal identity.

Japan has imported her food from the West, but not her vital nature. Japan cannot altogether lose and merge herself in the scientific paraphernalia she has acquired from the West and be turned into a mere borrowed machine. She has her own soul, which must assert itself over all her requirements. That she is capable of doing so, and that the process of assimilation is going on, have been amply proved by the signs of vigorous health that she exhibits. And I earnestly hope that Japan may never lose her faith in her own soul, in the mere pride of her foreign acquisition. For that pride itself is a humiliation, ultimately leading to poverty and weakness. It is the pride of the fop who sets more store on his new head-dress than on his head itself.

The whole world waits to see what this great eastern nation is going to do with the opportunities and responsibilities she has accepted from the hands of the modern time. If it be a mere reproduction of the West, then the great expectation she has raised will remain unfulfilled. For there are grave questions that western civilisation has presented before the world but not completely answered. The conflict between the individual and the state, labour and capital, the man and the woman; the conflict between the greed of material gain and the spiritual life of man, the organised selfishness of nations and the higher ideals of humanity; the conflict between all the ugly complexities inseparable from giant organisations of commerce and state and the natural instincts of man crying for simplicity and beauty and fulness of leisure – all these have to be brought to a harmony in a manner not yet dreamt of.

We have seen this great stream of civilisation choking itself from débris carried by its innumerable channels. We have seen that with all its vaunted love of humanity it has proved itself the greatest menace to Man, far worse than the sudden outbursts of nomadic barbarism from which men suffered in the early ages of history. We have seen that, in spite of its boasted love of freedom, it has produced worse forms of slavery than ever were current in earlier societies – slavery whose chains are unbreakable, either because they are unseen, or because they assume the names and appearance of freedom. We have seen, under the spell of its gigantic sordidness, man losing faith in all the heroic ideals of life which have made him great.

Therefore you cannot with a light heart accept the modern civilisation with all its tendencies, methods and structures, and dream that they are inevitable. You must apply your eastern mind, your spiritual strength, your love of simplicity, your recognition of social obligation, in order to cut out a new path for this great unwieldy car of progress, shrieking out its loud discords as it runs. You must minimise the immense sacrifice of man's life and freedom that it claims in its every movement. For generations you have felt and thought and worked, have enjoyed and worshipped in your own special manner; and this cannot be cast off like old clothes. It is in your blood, in the marrow of your bones, in the texture of your flesh, in the tissue of your brains; and it must modify everything you lay your hands upon, without your knowing, even against your wishes. Once you did solve the problems of man to your own satisfaction, you had your philosophy of life and evolved your own art of living. All this you must apply to the present situation, and out of it will arise a new creation and not a mere repetition, a creation which the soul of your people will own for itself and proudly offer to the world as its tribute to the welfare of man. Of all countries in Asia, here in Japan you have the freedom to use the materials you have gathered from the West according to your genius and your need. Therefore your responsibility is all the greater, for in your voice Asia shall answer the questions that Europe has submitted to the conference of Man. In your land the experiments will be carried on by which the East will change the aspects of modern civilisation, infusing life in it where it is a machine, substituting the human heart for cold expediency, not caring so much for power and success as for harmonious and living growth, for truth and beauty.

I cannot but bring to your mind those days when the whole of eastern Asia from Burma to Japan was united with India in the closest tie of friendship, the only natural tie which can exist between nations. There was a living communication of hearts, a nervous system evolved through which messages ran between us about the deepest needs of humanity. We did not stand in fear of each other; we had not to arm ourselves to keep each other in check; our relation was not that of self-interest, of exploration and spoliation of each other's pocket; ideas and ideals were exchanged, gifts of the highest love were offered and taken; no difference of languages and customs hindered us in approaching each other heart to heart; no pride of race or insolent consciousness of superiority, physical or mental, marred our relation; our arts and literatures put forth new leaves and flowers under the influence of this sunlight of united hearts, and races belonging to different lands and languages and histories acknowledged the highest unity of man and the deepest bond of love. May we not also remember that in those days of peace and goodwill, of men uniting for those supreme ends of life, your nature laid by for itself the balm of immotality which has helped your people to be born again in a new age, to be able to survive its old outworn structures and take on a new young body, to come out unscathed from the shock of the most wonderful revolution that the world has ever seen?

The political civilisation which has sprung up from the soil of Europe and is overrunning the whole world, like some prolific weed, is based upon exclusiveness. It is always watchful to keep the aliens at bay or to exterminate them. It is carnivorous and cannibalistic in its tendencies, it feeds upon the resources of other peoples and tries to swallow their whole future. It is always afraid of other races achieving eminence, naming it as a peril, and tries to thwart all symptoms of greatness outside its own boundaries, forcing down races of men who are weaker, to be eternally fixed in their weakness. Before this political civilisation came to its power and opened its hungry jaws wide enough to gulp down great continents of the earth, we had wars, pillages, changes of monarchy and consequent miseries, but never such a sight of fearful and hopeless voracity, such wholesale feeding of nation upon nation, such huge machines for turning great portions of the earth into mince-meat, never such terrible jealousies with all their ugly teeth and claws ready for tearing open each other's vitals. This political civilisation is scientific, not human. It is powerful because it concentrates all its forces upon one purpose, like a millionaire acquiring money at the cost of his soul. It betrays its trust, it weaves its meshes of

lies without shame, it enshrines gigantic idols of greed
in its temples, taking great pride in the costly ceremo-
nials of its worship, calling this patriotism. And it can
be safely prophesied that this cannot go on, for there
is a moral law in this world which has its application
both to individuals and to organised bodies of men.
You cannot go on violating these laws in the name of
your nation, yet enjoy their advantage as individuals.
This public sapping of ethical ideals slowly reacts upon
each member of society, gradually breeding weakness
where it is not seen, and causing that cynical distrust
of all things sacred in human nature, which is the
true symptom of senility. You must keep in mind
that this political civilisation, this creed of national
patriotism, has not been given a long trial. The lamp
of ancient Greece is extinct in the land where it was
first lighted; the power of Rome lies dead and buried
under the ruins of its vast empire. But the civilisation,
whose basis is society and the spiritual ideal of man,
is still a living thing in China and in India. Though it
may look feeble and small, judged by the standard of
the mechanical power of modern days, yet like small
seeds it still contains life and will sprout and grow,
and spread its beneficent branches, producing flowers
and fruits when its time comes and showers of grace
descend upon it from heaven. But ruins of skyscrapers
of power, and broken machinery of greed, even God's
rain is powerless to raise up again; for they were not of
life, but went against life as a whole – they are relics
of the rebellion that shattered itself to pieces against
the eternal.

But the charge is brought against us that the ideals
we cherish in the East are static, that they have not
the impetus in them to move, to open out new vistas of
knowledge and power, that the systems of philosophy
which are the mainstays of the time-worn civilisations

25

of the East despise all outward proofs, remaining stolidly satisfied in their subjective certainty. This proves that when our knowledge is vague we are apt to accuse of vagueness our object of knowledge itself. To a western observer our civilisation appears as all metaphysics, as to a deaf man piano-playing appears to be mere movements of fingers and no music. He cannot think that we have found some deep basis of reality upon which we have built our institutions.

Unfortunately all proofs of reality are in realisation. The reality of the scene before you depends only upon the fact that you can see, and it is difficult for us to prove to an unbeliever that our civilisation is not a nebulous system of abstract speculations, that it has achieved something which is a positive truth – a truth that can give man's heart its shelter and sustenance. It has evolved an inner sense – a sense of vision, the vision of the infinite reality in all finite things.

But he says, 'You do not make any progress; there is no movement in you.' I ask him, 'How do you know it? You have to judge progress according to its aim. A railway train makes its progress towards the terminus station – it is movement. But a full-grown tree has no definite movement of that kind; its progress is the inward progress of life. It lives, with its aspiration towards light tingling in its leaves and creeping in its silent sap.'

We also have lived for centuries; we still live, and we have our aspiration for a reality that has no end to its realisation – a reality that goes beyond death, giving it a meaning, that rises above all evils of life, bringing its peace and purity, its cheerful renunciation of self. The product of this inner life is a living product. It will be needed when the youth returns home weary and dust-laden, when the soldier is wounded, when the wealth is squandered away and pride is humbled, when man's heart cries for truth in the immensity of facts, and harmony in the contradiction of tendencies. Its value is not in its multiplication of materials, but in its spiritual fulfilment.

There are things that cannot wait. You have to rush and run and march if you must fight or take the best place in the market. You strain your nerves and are on the alert when you chase opportunities that are always on the wing. But there are ideals which do not play hide-and-seek with our life; they slowly grow from seed to flower, from flower to fruit; they require infinite space and heaven's light to mature, and the fruits that they produce can survive years of insult and neglect. The East with her ideals, in whose bosom are stored the ages of sunlight and silence of stars, can patiently wait till the West, hurrying after the expedient, loses breath and stops. Europe, while busily speeding to her engagements, disdainfully casts her glance from her carriage window at the reaper reaping his harvest in the field, and in her intoxication of speed cannot but think of him as slow and ever receding backwards. But the speed comes to its end; the engagement loses its meaning and the hungry heart clamours for food, till at last she comes to the lowly reaper reaping his harvest in the sun. For if the office cannot wait, or the buying and selling, or the craving for excitement, love waits, and beauty, and the wisdom of suffering and the fruits of patient devotion and reverent meekness of simple faith. And thus shall wait the East till her time comes.

I must not hesitate to acknowledge where Europe is great, for great she is without doubt. We cannot help loving her with all our heart and paying her the best homage of our admiration – the Europe who, in her literature and art, pours out an inexhaustible cascade of beauty and truth fertilising all countries and all time; the Europe who, with a mind which is titanic in its untiring power, is sweeping the height and the depth of the universe, winning her homage of knowledge from the infinitely great and the infinitely small, applying all the resources of her great intellect and heart in healing the sick and alleviating those miseries of man which up till now we were contented to accept in a spirit of hopeless resignation; the Europe who is making the earth yield more fruit than seemed possible, coaxing and compelling the great forces of nature into man's service. Such true greatness must have its motive power in spiritual strength. For only the spirit of man can defy all limitations, have faith in its ultimate success, throw its searchlight beyond the immediate and the apparent, gladly suffer martyrdom for ends which cannot be achieved in its lifetime and accept failure without acknowledging defeat. In the heart of Europe runs the purest stream of human love, of love of justice, of spirit of self-sacrifice for higher ideals. The Christian culture of centuries has sunk deep in her life's core. In Europe we have seen noble minds who have ever stood up for the rights of man irrespective of colour and creed; who have braved calumny and insult from their own people in fighting for humanity's cause and raising their voices against the mad orgies of militarism, against the rage for brutal retaliation or rapacity that sometimes takes possession of a whole people; who are always ready to make reparation for wrongs done in the past by their own nations and vainly attempt to stem the tide of cowardly injustice that flows unchecked because the resistance is weak and innocuous on the part of the injured. There are these knight-errants of modern Europe who have not lost their faith in the disinterested love of freedom, in the ideals which own no geographical boundaries or national self-seeking. These are there to prove that the fountainhead of the water of everlasting life has not run dry in Europe, and from thence she will have her rebirth time after time. Only there, where Europe is too consciously busy in building up her power, defying her deeper nature and mocking it, she is heaping up her iniquities to the sky, crying for God's vengeance and spreading the infection of ugliness, physical and moral, over the face of the earth with her heartless commerce heedlessly outraging man's sense of the beautiful and the good. Europe is supremely good in her beneficence where her face is turned to all humanity; and Europe is supremely evil in her maleficent aspect where her face is turned only upon her own interest, using all her power of greatness for ends which are against the infinite and eternal in Man.

Eastern Asia has been pursuing its own path, evolving its own civilisation, which was not political but social, not predatory and mechanically efficient but spiritual and based upon all the varied and deeper relations of humanity. The solutions of the life problems of peoples were thought out in seclusion and carried out behind the security of aloofness, where all the dynastic changes and foreign invasions hardly touched them. But now we are overtaken by the outside world, our seclusion is lost for ever. Yet this we must not regret, as a plant should never regret when the obscurity of its seed-time is broken. Now the time has come when we must make the world problem our own problem; we must bring the spirit of civilisation into harmony with the history of all nations of the earth; we must not, in foolish pride, still keep ourselves fast within the shell of the seed and the crust of the earth which protected and nourished our ideals; for these, the shell and the crust, were meant to be broken, so that life may spring up in all its vigour and beauty, bringing its offerings to the world in open light.

In this task of breaking the barrier and facing the world Japan has come out the first in the East. She has infused hope in the heart of all Asia. This hope provides the hidden fire which is needed for all works of creation. Asia now feels that she must prove her life by producing living work; she must not lie passively dormant, or feebly imitate the West, in the infatuation of fear and flattery. For this we offer our thanks to this Land of the Rising Sun and solemnly ask her to remember that she has the mission of the East to fulfil. She must infuse the sap of a fuller humanity into the heart of modern civilisation. She must never allow it to get choked with noxious undergrowth, but lead it up towards light and freedom, towards the pure air and broad space where it can receive, in the dawn of its day and the darkness of its night, heaven's inspiration. Let the greatness of her ideals become visible to all men like her snow-crowned Fuji rising from the heart of the country into the region of the infinite, supremely distinct from its surroundings, beautiful like a maiden in its magnificent sweep of curve, yet firm and strong and serenely majestic.

II

I have travelled in many countries and have met with men of all classes, but never in my travels did I feel the presence of the human so distinctly as in this land. In other great countries signs of man's power loomed large, and I saw vast organisations which showed efficiency in all their features. There, display and extravagance, in dress, in furniture, in costly entertainments, are startling. They seem to push you back into a corner, like a poor intruder at a feast; they are apt to make you envious, or take your breath away with amazement. There, you do not feel man as supreme; you are hurled against a stupendousness of things that alienate. But in Japan it is not the display of power or wealth that is the predominating element. You see everywhere emblems of love and admiration, and not mostly of ambition and greed. You see a people whose heart has come out and scattered itself in profusion in its commonest utensils of everyday life, in its social institutions, in its manners, which are carefully perfect, and in its dealings with things which are not only deft but graceful in every movement.

What has impressed me most in this country is the conviction that you have realised nature's secrets, not by methods of analytical knowledge, but by sympathy. You have known her language of lines, and music of colours, the symmetry in her irregularities, and the cadence in her freedom of movements; you have seen how she leads her immense crowds of things yet avoids all frictions, how the very conflicts in her creations break out in dance and music, how her exuberance has the aspect of the fulness of self-abandonment, and not a mere dissipation of display. You have discovered that nature reserves her power in forms of beauty; and it is this beauty which, like a mother, nourishes all the giant forces at her breast, keeping them in active vigour, yet in repose. You have known that energies of nature save themselves from wearing out by the rhythm of a perfect grace, and that she, with the tenderness of her curved lines, takes away fatigue from the world's muscles. I have felt that you have been able to assimilate these secrets into your life, and the truth which lies in the beauty of all things has passed into your souls. A mere knowledge of things can be had in a short enough time, but their spirit can only be acquired by centuries of training and self-control. Dominating nature from outside is a much simpler thing than making her your own

31

in love's delight, which is a work of true genius. Your race has shown that genius, not by acquirement but by creation, not by display of things but by manifestation of its own inner being. This creative power there is in all nations, and it is ever active in getting hold of men's natures and giving them a form according to its ideals. But here, in Japan, it seems to have achieved its success, and deeply sunk into the minds of all men, and permeated their muscles and nerves. Your instincts have become true, your senses keen, and your hands have acquired natural skill. The genius of Europe has given her people the power of organisation, which has specially made itself manifest in politics and commerce and in co-ordinating scientific knowledge. The genius of Japan has given you the vision of beauty in nature and the power of realising it in your life.

All particular civilisation is the interpretation of particular human experience. Europe seems to have felt emphatically the conflict of things in the universe, which can only be brought under control by conquest. Therefore she is ever ready for fight, and the best portion of her attention is occupied in organising forces. But Japan has felt, in her world, the touch of some presence, which has evoked in her soul a feeling of reverent adoration. She does not boast of her mastery of nature, but to her she brings, with infinite care and joy, her offerings of love. Her relationship with the world is the deeper relationship of heart. This spiritual bond of love she has established with the hills of her country, with the sea and the streams, with the forests in all their flowery moods and varied physiognomy of branches; she has taken into her heart all the rustling whispers and sighing of the woodlands and sobbing of the waves; the sun and the moon she has studied in all the modulations of their lights and shades, and she is glad to close her shops to greet the seasons in her orchards and gardens and cornfields. This opening of the heart to the soul of the world is not confined to a section of your privileged classes; it is not the forced product of exotic culture, but it belongs to all your men and women of all conditions. This experience of your soul, in meeting a personality in the heart of the world, has been embodied in your civilisation. It is a civilisation of human relationship. Your duty towards your state has naturally assumed the character of filial duty, your nation becoming one family with your Emperor as its head. Your national unity has not been evolved from the comradeship of arms for defensive and offensive purpose, or from partnership in raiding adventures, dividing among each member the danger and spoils of robbery. It is not an outcome of the necessity of organisation for some ulterior purpose, but it is an extension of the family and obligations of the heart in a wide field of space and time. The ideal of *maitri* is at the bottom of your culture – *maitri* with men and *maitri* with Nature. And the true expression of this love is in the language of beauty, which is so abundantly universal in this land. This is the reason why a stranger like myself, instead of feeling envy or humiliation before these manifestations of beauty, these creations of love, feels a readiness to participate in the joy and glory of such revealment of the human heart.

And this had made me all the more apprehensive of the change which threatens Japanese civilisation, as something like a menace to one's own person. For the huge heterogeneity of the modern age, whose only common bond is usefulness, is nowhere so pitifully exposed against the dignity and hidden power of reticent beauty as in Japan.

But the danger lies in this, that organised ugliness

storms the mind and carries the day by its mass, by its aggressive persistence, but its power of mockery directed against the deeper sentiments of the heart. Its harsh obtrusiveness makes it forcibly visible to us, overcoming our senses – and we bring sacrifices to its altar, as does a savage to the fetish which appears powerful because of its hideousness. Therefore its rivalry with things that are modest and profound and have the subtle delicacy of life is to be dreaded.

I am quite sure that there are men in your country who are not in sympathy with your inherited ideals, whose object is to gain and not to grow. They are loud in their boast that they have modernised Japan. While I agree with them so far as to say that the spirit of the race should harmonise with the spirit of the time, I must warn them that modernising is a mere affectation of modernism, just as an affectation of poesy is poetising. It is nothing but mimicry, only affectation is louder than the original, and it is too literal. One must bear in mind that those who have the true modern spirit need not modernise, just as those who are truly brave are not braggarts. Modernism is not in the dress of the Europeans, or in the hideous structures where their children are interned when they take their lessons, or in the square houses with flat, straight wall-surfaces, pierced with parallel lines of windows, where these people are caged in their lifetime; certainly modernism is not in their ladies' bonnets, carrying on them loads of incongruities. These are not modern, but merely European. True modernism is freedom of mind, not slavery of taste. It is independence of thought and action, not tutelage under European schoolmasters. It is science, but not its wrong application in life – a mere imitation of our science teachers who reduce it into a superstition, absurdly invoking its aid for all impossible purposes.

Life based upon mere science is attractive to some men, because it has all the characteristics of sport; it feigns seriousness, but is not profound. When you go a-hunting, the less pity you have the better; for your one object is to chase the game and kill it, to feel that you are the greater animal, that your method of destruction is thorough and scientific. And the life of science is that superficial life. It pursues success with skill and thoroughness, and takes no account of the higher nature of man. But those whose minds are crude enough to plan their lives upon the supposition that man is merely a hunter and his paradise the paradise of sportsmen will be rudely awakened in the midst of their trophies of skeletons and skulls.

I do not for a moment suggest that Japan should be unmindful of acquiring modern weapons of self-protection. But this should never be allowed to go beyond her instinct of self-preservation. She must know that the real power is not in the weapons themselves, but in the man who wields those weapons; and when he, in his eagerness for power, multiplies his weapons at the cost of his own soul, then it is he who is in even greater danger than his enemies.

Things that are living are so easily hurt; therefore they require protection. In nature, life protects itself within its coverings, which are built with life's own material. Therefore they are in harmony with life's growth, or else when the time comes they easily give way and are forgotten. The living man has his true protection in his spiritual ideals which have their vital connection with his life, and grow with his growth. But, unfortunately, all his armour is not living – some of it is made of steel, inert and mechanical. Therefore, while making use of it, man has to be careful to protect himself from its tyranny. If he is weak enough to grow smaller to fit himself to his covering, then it becomes a process of gradual suicide by shrinkage of the soul. And Japan must have a firm faith in the moral law of existence to be able to assert to herself that the western nations are following that path of suicide, where they are smothering their humanity under the immense weight of organisations in order to keep themselves in power and hold others in subjection.

What is dangerous for Japan is not the imitation of the outer features of the West, but the acceptance of the motive force of western nationalism as her own. Her social ideals are already showing signs of defeat at the hands of politics. I can see her motto, taken from science, 'Survival of the fittest', writ large at the entrance of her present day history – the motto whose meaning is, 'Help yourself, and never heed what it costs to others', the motto of the blind man who only believes in what he can touch, because he cannot see. But those who can see know that men are so closely knit that when you strike others the blow comes back to yourself. The moral law, which is the greatest discovery of man, is the discovery of this wonderful truth, that man becomes all the truer the more he realises himself in others. This truth has not only a subjective value, but is manifested in every department of our life. And nations who sedulously cultivate moral blindness as the cult of patriotism will end their existence in a sudden and violent death. In past ages we had foreign invasions, but they never touched the soul of the people deeply. They were merely the outcome of individual ambitions. The people themselves, being free from the responsibilities of the baser and more heinous side of those adventures, had all the advantage of the heroic and the human disciplines derived from them. This developed their unflinching loyalty, their single-minded devotion to the obligations of honour, their power of complete self-surrender and fearless acceptance of death and danger. Therefore the ideals, whose seats were in the hearts of the people, would not undergo any serious change owing to the policies adopted by the kings or generals. But now, where the spirit of western nationalism prevails, the whole people is being taught from boyhood to foster hatreds and ambitions by all kinds of means – by the manufacture of half-truths and untruths in history, by persistent misrepresentation of other races and the culture of unfavourable sentiments towards them, by setting up memorials of events, very often false, which for the sake of humanity should be speedily forgotten, thus continually brewing evil menace towards neighbours and nations other than their own. This is poisoning the very fountainhead of humanity. It is discrediting the ideals which were born of the lives of men who were our greatest and best. It is holding up gigantic selfishness as the one universal religion for all nations of the world. We can take anything else from the hands of science, but not this elixir of moral death. Never think for a moment that the hurts you inflict upon other races will not infect you, or that the enmities you sow around your homes will be a wall of protection to you for all time to come. To imbue the minds of the whole people with an abnormal vanity of its own superiority, to teach it to take pride in its moral callousness and ill-begotten wealth, to perpetuate the humiliation of defeated nations by exhibiting trophies won from war, and using these in schools in order to breed in children's minds contempt for others, is imitating the West where she has a festering sore, whose swelling is a swelling of disease eating into its vitality.

Our food crops, which are necessary for our sustenance, are products of centuries of selection and

care. But the vegetation, which we have not to trans-
form into our lives, does not require the patient
thoughts of generations. It is not easy to get rid of
weeds; but it is easy, by process of neglect, to ruin
your food crops and let them revert to their primitive
state of wildness. Likewise the culture, which has
so kindly adapted itself to your soil – so intimate
with life, so human – not only needed tilling and
weeding in past ages, but still needs anxious work
and watching. What is merely modern – as science
and methods of organisation – can be transplanted;
but what is vitally human has fibres so delicate,
and roots so numerous and far-reaching, that it dies
when moved from the soil. Therefore I am afraid of
the rude pressure of the political ideals of the West
upon your own. In political civilisation, the state
is an abstraction and the relationship of men utili-
tarian. Because it has no root in sentiments, it is
so dangerously easy to handle. Half a century has
been enough for you to master this machine; and
there are men among you whose fondness for it
exceeds their love for the living ideals, which were
born with the birth of your nation and nursed in your
centuries. It is like a child who, in the excitement
of his play, imagines he likes his play-things better
than his mother.

Where man is at his greatest, he is unconscious.
Your civilisation, whose mainspring is the bond of
human relationship, has been nourished in the depth
of a healthy life beyond reach of prying self-analysis.
But a mere political relationship is all-conscious; it
is an eruptive inflammation of aggressiveness. It has
forcibly burst upon your notice. And the time has come
when you have to be roused into full consciousness of
the truth by which you live, so that you may not be
taken unawares. The past has been God's gift to you;

about the present, you must make your own choice.

So the questions you have to put to yourselves are these: 'Have we read the world wrong, and based our relation to it upon an ignorance of human nature? Is the instinct of the West right, where she builds her national welfare behind the barricade of a universal distrust of humanity?'

You must have detected a strong accent of fear whenever the West has discussed the possibility of the rise of an eastern race. The reason of it is this, that the power by whose help she thrives is an evil power; so long as it is held on her own side she can be safe, while the rest of the world trembles. The vital ambition of the present civilisation of Europe is to have the exclusive possession of the devil. All her armaments and diplomacy are directed upon this one object. But these costly rituals for invocation of the evil spirit lead through a path of prosperity to the brink of cataclysm. The furies of terror, which the West has let loose upon God's world, come back to threaten herself and goad her into preparations of more and more frightfulness; this gives her no rest, and makes her forget all else but the perils that she causes to others and incurs herself. To the worship of this devil of politics she sacrifices other countries as victims. She feeds upon their dead flesh and grows fat upon it, so long as the carcasses remain fresh – but they are sure to rot at last, and the dead will take their revenge by spreading pollution far and wide and poisoning the vitality of the feeder. Japan had all her wealth of humanity, her harmony of heroism and beauty, her depth of self-control and richness of self-expression; yet the western nations felt no respect for her till she proved that the bloodhounds of Satan are not only bred in the kennels of Europe but can also be domesticated in Japan and fed with man's miseries. They admit Japan's equality with themselves,

only when they know that Japan also possesses the
key to open the floodgate of hell-fire upon the fair
earth whenever she chooses, and can dance in their
own measure the devil dance of pillage, murder and
ravishment of innocent women, while the world goes
to ruin. We know that, in the early stage of man's
moral immaturity, he only feels reverence for the
god whose malevolence he dreads. But is this the
ideal of man which we can look up to with pride:
after centuries of civilisation nations fearing each
other like the prowling wild beasts of the night-
time; shutting their doors of hospitality; combining
only for purpose of aggression or defence; hiding
in their holes their trade secrets, state secrets, secrets
of their armaments; making peace-offerings to each
other's barking dogs with the meat which does not
belong to them; holding down fallen races which
struggle to stand upon their feet; with their right
hands dispensing religion to weaker peoples, while
robbing them with their left – is there anything in
this to make us envious? Are we to bend our knees
to the spirit of this nationalism, which is sowing
broadcast over all the world seeds of fear, greed,
suspicion, unashamed lies of its diplomacy, and unc-
tuous lies of its profession of peace and goodwill
and universal brotherhood of Man? Can our minds
be free from doubt when we rush to the western
market to buy this foreign product in exchange for
our own inheritance? I am aware how difficult it
is to know one's self; and the man who is intoxi-
cated furiously denies his drunkenness; yet the West
herself is anxiously thinking of her problems and
trying experiments. But she is like a glutton, who
has not the heart to give up his intemperance in
eating, and fondly clings to the hope he can cure
his nightmares of indigestion by medicine. Europe

is not ready to give up her political inhumanity, with all the baser passions of man attendant upon it; she believes only in modification of systems, and not in change of heart.

We are willing to buy their machine-made systems, not with our hearts, but with our brains. We shall try them and build sheds for them, but not enshrine them in our homes or temples. There are races who worship the animals they kill; we can buy meat from them when we are hungry, but not the worship which goes with the killing. We must not vitiate our children's minds with the superstition that business is business, war is war, politics is politics. We must know that man's business has to be more than mere business, and so should be his war and politics. You had your own industry in Japan; how scrupulously honest and true it was, you can see by its products – by their grace and strength, their conscientiousness in details, where they can hardly be observed. But the tidal wave of falsehood has swept over your land from that part of the world where business is business, and honesty is followed merely as a best policy. Have you never felt shame when you see the trade advertisements, not only plastering the whole town with lies and exaggerations, but invading the green fields, where the peasants do their honest labour, and the hill-tops, which greet the first pure light of the morning? It is so easy to dull our sense of honour and delicacy of mind with constant abrasion, while falsehoods stalk abroad with proud steps in the name of trade, politics and patriotism, that any protest against their perpetual intrusion into our lives is considered to be sentimentalism, unworthy of true manliness.

And it has come to pass that the children of those heroes who would keep their word at the point of death, who would disdain to cheat men for vulgar profit, who even in their fight would much rather court defeat than be dishonourable, have become energetic in dealing with falsehoods and do not feel humiliated by gaining advantage from them. And this has been effected by the charm of the word 'modern'. But if undiluted utility be modern, beauty is of all ages; if mean selfishness be modern, the human ideals are no new inventions. And we must know for certain that however modern may be the proficiency which cripples man for the sake of methods and machines, it will never live to be old.

But while trying to free our minds from the arrogant claims of Europe and to help ourselves out of the quicksands of our infatuation, we may go to the other extreme and bind ourselves with a wholesale suspicion of the West. The reaction of disillusionment is just as unreal as the first shock of illusion. We must try to come to that normal state of mind by which we can clearly discern our own danger and avoid it without being unjust towards the source of that danger. There is always the natural temptation in us of wishing to pay back Europe in her own coin, and return contempt for contempt and evil for evil. But that again would be to imitate Europe in one of her worst features, which comes out in her behaviour to people whom she describes as yellow or red, brown or black. And this is a point on which we in the East have to acknowledge our guilt and own that our sin has been as great, if not greater, when we insulted humanity by treating with utter disdain and cruelty men who belonged to a particular creed, colour or caste. It is really because we are afraid of our own weakness, which allows itself to be overcome by the sight of power, that we try to substitute for it another weakness which makes itself blind to the glories of the

West. When we truly know that Europe which is great and good, we can effectively save ourselves from the Europe which is mean and grasping. It is easy to be unfair in one's judgement when one is faced with human miseries – and pessimism is the result of building theories while the mind is suffering. To despair of humanity is only possible if we lose faith in truth which brings to it strength, when its defeat is greatest, and calls out new life from the depth of its destruction. We must admit that there is a living soul in the West which is struggling unobserved against the hugeness of the organisations under which men, women and children are being crushed, and whose mechanical necessities are ignoring laws that are spiritual and human – the soul whose sensibilities refuse to be dulled completely by dangerous habits of heedlessness in dealings with races for whom it lacks natural sympathy. The West could never have risen to the eminence she has reached if her strength were merely the strength of the brute or of the machine. The divine in her heart is suffering from the injuries inflicted by her hands upon the world – and from this pain of her higher nature flows the secret balm which will bring healing to these injuries. Time after time she has fought against herself and has undone the chains which with her own hands she fastened round helpless limbs; and though she forced poison down the throat of a great nation at the point of the sword for gain of money, she herself woke up to withdraw from it, to wash her hands clean again. This shows hidden springs of humanity in spots which look dead and barren. It proves that the deeper truth in her nature, which can survive such a career of cruel cowardliness, is not greed, but reverence for unselfish ideals. It would be altogether unjust, both to us and to Europe, to say that she has fascinated the modern eastern mind by the mere exhibition of her power. Through the smoke of cannons and dust of markets the light of her moral nature has shone bright, and she has brought to us the ideal of ethical freedom, whose foundation lies deeper than social conventions and whose province of activity is world-wide.

The East has instinctively felt, even through her aversion, that she has a great deal to learn from Europe, not merely about the materials of power, but about its inner source, which is of the mind and of the moral nature of man. Europe has been teaching us the higher obligations of public good above those of the family and the clan, and the sacredness of law, which makes society independent of individual caprice, secures for it continuity of progress, and guarantees justice to all men of all positions in life. Above all things Europe has held high before our minds the banner of liberty, through centuries of martyrdom and achievement – liberty of conscience, liberty of thought and action, liberty in the ideals of art and literature. And because Europe has won our deep respect, she has become so dangerous for us where she is turbulently weak and false – dangerous like poison when it is served along with our best food. There is one safety for us upon which we hope we may count, and that is that we can claim Europe herself as our ally in our resistance to her temptations and to her violent encroachments; for she has ever carried her own standard of perfection, by which we can measure her falls and gauge her degrees of failure, by which we can call her before her own tribunal and put her to shame – the shame which is the sign of the true pride of nobleness.

But our fear is that the poison may be more powerful than the food, and what is strength in her today may not be a sign of health, but the contrary; for it may be temporarily caused by the upsetting of the balance of life. Our fear is that evil has a fateful fascination when it assumes dimensions which are colossal – and though at last it is sure to lose its centre of gravity by its abnormal disproportion, the mischief which it creates before its fall may be beyond reparation.

Therefore I ask you to have the strength of faith and clarity of mind to know for certain that the lumbering structure of modern progress, riveted by the iron bolts of efficiency, which runs upon the wheels of ambition, cannot hold together for long. Collisions are certain to occur, for it has to travel upon organised lines; it is too heavy to choose its own course freely, and once it is off the rails its endless train of vehicles is dislocated. A day will come when it will fall in a heap of ruin and cause serious obstruction to the traffic of the world. Do we not see signs of this even now? Does not the voice come to us through the din of war, the shrieks of hatred, the wailings of despair, through the churning of the unspeakable filth which has been accumulating for ages in the bottom of this nationalism – the voice which cries to our soul that the tower of national self-ishness, which goes by the name of patriotism, which has raised its banner of treason against heaven, must totter and fall with a crash, weighed down by its own bulk, its flag kissing the dust, its light extinguished? My brothers, when the red light of conflagration sends up its crackle of laughter to the stars, keep your faith upon those stars and not upon the fire of destruction. For when the conflagration consumes itself and dies down, leaving its memorial in ashes, the eternal light will again shine in the East – the East which has been the birthplace of the morning sun of man's history. And who knows if that day has not already dawned, and the sun not risen, in the easternmost horizon of Asia? And

I offer, as did my ancestor *rishis*, my salutation to that sunrise of the East, which is destined once again to illumine the whole world.

I know my voice is too feeble to raise itself above the uproar of this bustling time, and it is easy for any street urchin to fling against me the epithet of 'unpractical'. It will stick to my coat-tail, never to be washed away, effectively excluding me from the consideration of all respectable persons. I know what a risk one runs from the vigorously athletic crowds in being styled an idealist in these days, when thrones have lost their dignity and prophets have become an anachronism, when the sound that drowns all voices is the noise of the market-place. Yet when, one day, standing on the outskirts of Yokohama town bristling with its display of modern miscellanies, I watched the sunset in your southern sea, and saw its peace and majesty among your pine-clad hills – with the great Fujiyama growing faint against the golden horizon, like a god overcome with his own radiance – the music of eternity welled up through the evening silence, and I felt that the sky and the earth and the lyrics of the dawn and the dayfall are with the poets and idealists, and not with the marketmen robustly contemptuous of all sentiment – that, after all the forgetfulness of his divinity, man will remember again that heaven is always in touch with his world, which can never be abandoned for good to the hounding wolves of the modern era, scenting human blood and howling to the skies.

Nationalism in the West

Man's history is being shaped according to the difficulties it encounters. These have offered us problems and claimed their solutions from us, the penalty of non-fulfilment being death or degradation.

These difficulties have been different in different peoples of the earth, and in the manner of our overcoming them lies our distinction.

The Scythians of the earlier period of Asiatic history had to struggle with the scarcity of their natural resources. The easiest solution that they could think of was to organise their whole population, men, women, and children, into bands of robbers. And they were irresistible to those who were chiefly engaged in the constructive work of social co-operation.

But fortunately for man the easiest path is not his truest path. If his nature were not as complex as it is, if it were as simple as that of a pack of hungry wolves, then, by this time, those hordes of marauders would have overrun the whole earth. But man, when confronted with difficulties, has to acknowledge that he is man, that he has his responsibilities to the higher faculties of his nature, by ignoring which he may achieve success that is immediate, perhaps, but that will become a death-trap to him. For what are obstacles to the lower creatures are opportunities to the higher life of man.

To India has been given her problem from the beginning of history – it is the race problem. Races ethnologically different have in this country come into close contact. This fact has been and still continues to be the most important one in our history. It is our mission to face it and prove our humanity by dealing with it in the fullest truth. Until we fulfil our mission all other benefits will be denied us.

There are other peoples in the world who have to overcome obstacles in their physical surroundings, or the menace of their powerful neighbours. They have organised their power till they are not only reason-ably free from the tyranny of Nature and human neighbours, but have a surplus of it left in their hands to employ against others. But in India, our difficulties being internal, our history has been the history of continual social adjustment and not that of organised power for defence and aggression.

Neither the colourless vagueness of cosmopolitan-ism, nor the fierce self-idolatry of nation-worship, is the goal of human history. And India has been trying to accomplish her task through social regulation of differences on the one hand, and the spiritual rec-ognition of unity on the other. She has made grave errors in setting up the boundary walls too rigidly between races, in perpetuating in her classifications the results of inferiority; often she has crippled her children's minds and narrowed their lives in order to fit them into her social forms, but for centuries new experiments have been made and adjustments carried out.

Her mission has been like that of a hostess who

has to provide proper accommodation for numerous guests, whose habits and requirements are different from one another. This gives rise to infinite complexities whose solution depends not merely upon tactfulness but upon sympathy and true realisation of the unity of man. Towards this realisation have worked, from the early time of the *Upanishads** up to the present moment, a series of great spiritual teachers, whose one object has been to set at naught all differences of man by the overflow of our consciousness of God. In fact, our history has not been of the rise and fall of kingdoms, of fights for political supremacy. In our country records of these days have been despised and forgotten, for they in no way represent the true history of our people. Our history is that of our social life and attainment of spiritual ideals.

But we feel that our task is not yet done. The world-flood has swept over our country, new elements have been introduced, and wider adjustments are waiting to be made.

We feel this all the more because the teaching and example of the West have entirely run counter to what we think was given to India to accomplish. In the West the national machinery of commerce and politics turns out neatly compressed bales of humanity which have their use and high market value; but they are bound in iron hoops, labelled and separated off with scientific care and precision. Obviously God made man to be human, but this modern product has such marvellous square-cut finish, savouring of gigantic manufacture, that the Creator will find it difficult to recognise it as a thing of spirit and a creature made in His own divine image.

But I am anticipating. What I was about to say

* About 200 prose and verse treatises on metaphysical philosophy, dating from around 400 BC.

is this. Take it in whatever spirit you like, here is India, of about fifty centuries at least, who tried to live peacefully and think deeply, the India devoid of all politics, the India of no nations, whose one ambition has been to know this world as of soul, to live here every moment of her life in the meek spirit of adoration, in the glad consciousness of an eternal and personal relationship with it. It was upon this remote portion of humanity, childlike in its manner, with the wisdom of the old, that the Nation of the West burst in.

Through all the fights and intrigues and deceptions of her earlier history India had remained aloof. Because her homes, her fields, her temples of worship, her schools, where her teachers and students lived together in the atmosphere of simplicity and devotion and learning, her village self-government with its simple laws and peaceful administration – all these truly belonged to her. But her thrones were not her concern. They passed over her head like clouds, now tinged with purple gorgeousness, now black with the threat of thunder. Often they brought devastations in their wake, but they were like catastrophes of nature whose traces are soon forgotten.

But this time it was different. It was not a mere drift over her surface of life – drift of cavalry and foot soldiers, richly caparisoned elephants, white tents and canopies, strings of patient camels bearing the loads of royalty, bands of kettle-drums and flutes, marble domes of mosques, palaces and tombs, like the bubbles of the foaming wine of extravagance; stories of treachery and loyal devotion, of changes of fortune, of dramatic surprises of fate. This time it was the Nation of the West driving its tentacles of machinery deep down into the soil.

Therefore I say to you, it is we who are called as witnesses to give evidence as to what our Nation has been to humanity. We had known the hordes of Mughals and Pathans who invaded India, but we had known them as human races, with their own religions and customs, likes and dislikes – we had never known them as a nation. We loved and hated them as the occasions arose; we fought for them and against them, talked with them in a language which was theirs as well as our own, and guided the destiny of the Empire in which we had our active share. But this time we had to deal, not with kings, not with human races, but with a nation – we, who are no nation ourselves.

Now let us, from our own experience, answer the question: what is this Nation?

A nation, in the sense of the political and economic union of a people, is that aspect which a whole population assumes when organised for a mechanical purpose. Society as such has no ulterior purpose. It is an end in itself. It is a spontaneous self-expression of man as a social being. It is a natural regulation of human relationships, so that men can develop ideals of life in co-operation with one another. It has also a political side, but this is only for a special purpose. It is for self-preservation. It is merely the side of power, not of human ideals. And in the early days it had its separate place in society, restricted to the professionals. But when with the help of science and the perfecting of organisation this power begins to grow and brings in harvests of wealth, then it crosses its boundaries with amazing rapidity. For then it goads all its neighbouring societies with greed of material prosperity, and consequent mutual jealousy, and by the fear of each other's growth into powerfulness. The time comes when it can stop no longer, for the competition grows keener, organisation grows vaster, and selfishness attains supremacy. Trading upon the greed and fear of man, it occupies more and more space in society, and at last becomes its ruling force.

It is just possible that you have lost through habit the consciousness that the living bonds of society are breaking up, and giving place to merely mechanical organisation. But one sees signs of it everywhere. It is owing to this that war has been declared between man and woman, because the natural thread is snapping which holds them together in harmony; because man is driven to professionalism, producing wealth for himself and others, continually turning the wheel of power for his own sake or for the sake of the universal officialdom, leaving woman alone to wither and to die or to fight her own battle unaided. And thus there, where co-operation is natural, has intruded competition. The very psychology of men and women about their mutual relation is changing and becoming the psychology of the primitive fighting elements, rather than of humanity seeking its completeness through the union based upon mutual self-surrender. For the elements which have lost their living bond of reality have lost the meaning of their existence. Like gaseous particles forced into a too narrow space, they come in continual conflict with each other till they burst the very arrangement which holds them in bondage.

Then look at those who call themselves anarchists, who resent the imposition of power, in any form whatever, upon the individual. The only reason for this is that power has become too abstract – it is a scientific product made in the political laboratory of the Nation, through the dissolution of personal humanity.

And what is the meaning of these strikes in the economic world, which like the prickly shrubs in a barren soil shoot up with renewed vigour each time they are cut down? What but that the wealth-producing mechanism is incessantly growing into vast stature, out of proportion to all other needs of society, and the full reality of man is more and more crushed under its weight? This state of things inevitably gives rise to eternal feuds among the elements freed from the wholeness and wholesomeness of human ideals, and interminable economic war is waged between capital and labour. For greed of wealth and power can never have a limit, and compromise of self-interest can never attain the final spirit of reconciliation. They must go on breeding jealousy and suspicion to the end – the end which only comes through some sudden catastrophe or a spiritual rebirth.

When this organisation of politics and commerce, whose other name is the Nation, becomes all-powerful at the cost of the harmony of the higher social life, then it is an evil day for humanity. When a father becomes a gambler and his obligations to his family take the secondary place in his mind, then he is no longer a man, but an automaton led by the power of greed. Then he can do things which, in his normal state of mind, he would be ashamed to do. It is the same thing with society. When it allows itself to be turned into a perfect organisation of power, then there are few crimes it is unable to perpetrate, because success is the object and justification of a machine, while goodness only is the end and purpose of man. When this engine of organisation begins to attain a vast size, and those who are mechanics are made into parts of the machine, then the personal man is eliminated to a phantom, everything becomes a revolution of policy carried out by the human parts of the machines, with no twinge of pity or moral responsibility. It may happen that even through this apparatus the moral nature of man tries to assert itself, but the whole series of ropes and pulleys creak and cry, the forces of the human heart become entangled among the forces of the human automaton, and only with difficulty can the moral purpose transmit itself into some tortured shape of result.

This abstract being, the Nation, is ruling India. We have seen in our country some brand of tinned food advertised as entirely made and packed without being touched by hand. This description applies to the governing of India, which is as little touched by the human hand as possible. The governors need not know our language, need not come into personal touch with us except as officials; they can aid or hinder our aspirations from a disdainful distance, they can lead us on a certain path of policy and then pull us back again with the manipulation of office red tape. The newspapers of England, in whose columns London street accidents are recorded with some decency of pathos, need take but the scantiest notice of calamities which happen in India over areas of land sometimes larger than the British Isles.

But we, who are governed, are not a mere abstraction. We, on our side, are individuals with living sensibilities. What comes to us in the shape of a mere bloodless policy may pierce into the very core of our life, may threaten the whole future of our people with a perpetual helplessness of emasculation, and yet may never touch the chord of humanity on the other side, or touch it in the most inadequately feeble manner. Such wholesale and universal acts of fearful responsibility man can never perform, with such a degree of systematic unawareness, where he is an individual human being. These only become possible where the man is represented by an octopus of abstractions, sending out its wriggling arms in all directions of space, and fixing its innumerable suckers even into the far-away future. In this reign of the nation, the governed are pursued by suspicions; and these are the suspicions of a tremendous mass of organised brain and muscle. Punishments are meted out which leave a trail of miseries across a large bleeding tract of the human heart, but these punishments are dealt by a mere abstract force in which a whole population of a distant country has lost its human personality.

I have not come here, however, to discuss the question as it affects my own country, but as it affects the future of all humanity. It is not a question of the British government, but of government by the Nation – the Nation which is the organised self-interest of a whole people, where it is least human and least spiritual. Our only intimate experience of the Nation is with the British Nation, and as far as the government by the Nation goes there are reasons to believe that it is one of the best. Then, again, we have to consider that the West is necessary to the East. We are complementary to each other because of our different outlooks upon life which have given us different aspects of truth. Therefore if it be true that the spirit of the West has come upon our fields in the guise of a storm it is nevertheless scattering living seeds that are immortal. And when in India we become able to assimilate in our life what is permanent in western civilisation we shall be in a position to bring about a reconciliation of these two great worlds. Then will come to an end the one-sided dominance which is galling. What is more, we have to recognise that the history of India does not belong to one particular race but to a process of creation to which various races of the world contributed – the Dravidians and the Aryans, the ancient Greeks and the Persians, the Mohammedans of the West and those of central Asia. Now at last has come the turn of the English to become true to this history and bring to it the tribute of their life, and we neither have the right nor the power to exclude this people from the building of the destiny of India. Therefore what I say about the

Nation has more to do with the history of Man than specially with that of India.

This history has come to a stage when the moral man, the complete man, is more and more giving way, almost without knowing it, to make room for the political and the commercial man, the man of the limited purpose. This process, aided by the wonderful progress in science, is assuming gigantic proportion and power, causing the upset of man's moral balance, obscuring his human side under the shadow of soulless organisation. We have felt its iron grip at the root of our life, and for the sake of humanity we must stand up and give warning to all, that this nationalism is a cruel epidemic of evil that is sweeping over the human world of the present age and eating into its moral vitality.

I have a deep love and a great respect for the British race as human beings. It has produced great-hearted men, thinkers of great thoughts, doers of great deeds. It has given rise to a great literature. I know that these people love justice and freedom, and hate lies. They are clean in their minds, frank in their manners, true in their friendships; in their behaviour they are honest and reliable. The personal experience which I have had of their literary men has roused my admiration not merely for their power of thought or expression but for their chivalrous humanity. We have felt the greatness of this people as we feel the sun; but as for the Nation, it is for us a thick mist of a stifling nature covering the sun itself.

This government by the Nation is neither British nor anything else; it is an applied science and therefore more or less similar in its principles wherever it is used. It is like a hydraulic press, whose pressure is impersonal, and on that account completely effective. The amount of its power may vary in different engines. Some may even be driven by hand, thus leaving a margin of comfortable looseness in their tension, but in spirit and in method their differences are small. Our government might have been Dutch, or French, or Portuguese, and its essential features would have remained much the same as they are now. Only perhaps, in some cases, the organisation might not have been so densely perfect, and therefore some shreds of the human might still have been clinging to the wreck, allowing us to deal with something which resembles our own throbbing heart.

Before the Nation came to rule over us we had other governments which were foreign, and these, like all governments, had some element of the machine in them. But the difference between them and the government by the Nation is like the difference between the hand-loom and the power-loom. In the products of the hand-loom the magic of man's living fingers finds its expression, and its hum harmonises with the music of life. But the power-loom is relentlessly lifeless and accurate and monotonous in its production.

We must admit that during the personal government of former days there have been instances of tyranny, injustice, and extortion. They caused sufferings and unrest from which we are glad to be rescued. The protection of law is not only a boon, but it is a valuable lesson to us. It is teaching us the discipline which is necessary for the stability of civilisation and for continuity of progress. We are realising through it that there is a universal standard of justice to which all men, irrespective of their caste and colour, have their equal claim.

This reign of law in our present government in India has established order in this vast land inhabited by peoples different in their races and customs. It has made it possible for these peoples to come in closer touch with one another and cultivate a communion of aspiration.

But this desire for a common bond of comradeship among the different races of India has been the work of the spirit of the West, not that of the Nation of the West. Wherever in Asia the people have received the true lesson of the West it is in spite of the western Nation. Only because Japan had been able to resist the dominance of this western Nation could she acquire the benefit of western civilisation in fullest measure. Though China has been poisoned at the very spring of her moral and physical life by this Nation, her struggle to receive the best lessons of the West may yet be successful if not hindered by the Nation. It was only the other day that Persia woke up from her age-long sleep at the call of the West to be instantly trampled into stillness by the Nation. The same phenomenon prevails in this country also, where the people are hospitable, but the Nation has proved itself to be otherwise, making an Eastern guest feel humiliated to stand before you as a member of the humanity of his own motherland.

In India we are suffering from this conflict between the spirit of the West and the Nation of the West. The benefit of western civilisation is doled out to us in a miserly measure by the Nation, which tries to regulate the degree of nutrition as near the zero-point of vitality as possible. The portion of education allotted to us is so raggedly insufficient that it ought to outrage the sense of decency of western humanity. We have seen in these countries how the people are encouraged and trained and given every facility to fit themselves for the great movements of commerce and industry spreading over the world, while in India the only assistance we get is merely to be jeered at by the Nation for lagging behind. While depriving us of our opportunities and reducing our education to the minimum required for conducting a foreign government, this Nation pacifies its conscience by calling us names, by sedulously giving currency to the arrogant cynicism that the East is east and the West is west and never the twain shall meet. If we must believe our schoolmaster in his taunt that, after nearly two centuries of his tutelage, India not only remains unfit for self-government but unable to display originality in her intellectual attainments, must we ascribe it to something in the nature of western culture and our inherent incapacity to receive it or to the judicious niggardliness of the Nation that has taken upon itself the white man's burden of civilising the East? That Japanese people have some qualities which we lack we may admit, but that our intellect is naturally unproductive compared to theirs we cannot accept even from them whom it is dangerous for us to contradict.

The truth is that the spirit of conflict and conquest is at the origin and in the centre of western nationalism; its basis is not social co-operation. It has evolved a perfect organisation of power, but not spiritual idealism. It is like the pack of predatory creatures that must have its victims. With all its heart it cannot bear to see its hunting-grounds converted into cultivated fields. In fact, these nations are fighting among themselves for the extension of their victims and their reserve forests. Therefore the western Nation acts like a dam to check the free flow of western civilisation into the country of the No-Nation. Because this civilisation is the civilisation of power, therefore it is exclusive; it is naturally unwilling to open its sources of power to those whom it has selected for its purposes of exploitation.

But all the same, moral law is the law of humanity, and the exclusive civilisation which thrives upon others who are barred from its benefit carries its own

59

death-sentence in its moral limitations. The slavery that it gives rise to unconsciously drains its own love of freedom dry. The helplessness with which it weighs down its world of victims exerts its force of gravitation every moment upon the power that creates it. And the greater part of the world which is being denuded of its self-sustaining life by the Nation will one day become the most terrible of all its burdens, ready to drag it down into the bottom of destruction. Whenever the Power removes all checks from its path to make its career easy, it triumphantly rides into its ultimate crash of death. Its moral brake becomes slacker every day without its knowing it, and its slippery path of ease becomes its path of doom.

Of all things in western civilisation, those which this western Nation has given us in a most generous measure are law and order. While the small feeding-bottle of our education is nearly dry, and sanitation sucks its own thumb in despair, the military organisation, the magisterial offices, the police, the Criminal Investigation Department, the secret spy system, attain to an abnormal girth in their waists, occupying every inch of our country. This is to maintain order. But is not this order merely a negative good? Is it not for giving people's life greater opportunities for the freedom of development? Its perfection is the perfection of an egg-shell, whose true value lies in the security it affords to the chick and its nourishment and not in the convenience it offers to the person at the breakfast table. Mere administration is unproductive; it is not creative, not being a living thing. It is a steam-roller, formidable in its weight and power, having its uses, but it does not help the soil to become fertile. When after its enormous toil it comes to offer us its boon of peace we can but murmur under our breath that 'peace is

good, but not more so than life, which is God's own
great boon'.

On the other hand, our former governments were
woefully lacking in many of the advantages of the
modern government. But because those were not the
governments by the Nation, their texture was loosely
woven, leaving big gaps through which our own life
sent its threads and imposed its designs. I am quite
sure in those days we had things that were extremely
distasteful to us. But we know that when we walk
barefooted upon ground strewn with gravel, our feet
come gradually to adjust themselves to the caprices
of the inhospitable earth; while if the tiniest particle
of gravel finds its lodgement inside our shoes we can
never forget and forgive its intrusion. And these shoes
are the government by the Nation – it is tight, it regulates our steps with a closed-up system, within which
our feet have only the slightest liberty to make their
own adjustments. Therefore, when you produce your
statistics to compare the number of gravels which our
feet had to encounter in former days with the paucity
in the present regime, they hardly touch the real point.
It is not a question of the number of outside obstacles
but the comparative powerlessness of the individual to
cope with them. This narrowness of freedom is an evil
which is more radical, not because of its quantity but
because of its nature. And we cannot but acknowledge
this paradox: that while the spirit of the West marches
under its banner of freedom, the Nation of the West
forges its iron chains of organisation which are the
most relentless and unbreakable that have ever been
manufactured in the whole history of man.

When the humanity of India was not under the
government of the Organisation, the elasticity of
change was great enough to encourage men of power
and spirit to feel that they had their destinies in their

own hands. The hope of the unexpected was never absent, and a freer play of imagination, on the part of both the governor and the governed, had its effect in the making of history. We were not confronted with a future, which was a dead white wall of granite blocks eternally guarding against the expression and extension of our own powers, the hopelessness of which lies in the reason that these powers are becoming atrophied at their very roots by the scientific process of paralysis. For every single individual in the country of the No-Nation is completely in the grip of a whole nation, whose tireless vigilance, being the vigilance of a machine, has not the human power to overlook or to discriminate. At the least pressing of its button the monster organisation becomes all eyes, whose ugly stare of inquisitiveness cannot be avoided by a single person amongst the immense multitude of the ruled. At the least turn of its screw, by the fraction of an inch, the grip is tightened to the point of suffocation around every man, woman and child of a vast population, for whom no escape is imaginable in their own country or even in any country outside their own.

It is the continual and stupendous dead pressure of the inhuman upon the living human under which the modern world is groaning. Not merely the subject races, but you who live under the delusion that you are free, are every day sacrificing your freedom and humanity to this fetish of nationalism, living in the dense poisonous atmosphere of world-wide suspicion and greed and panic.

I have seen in Japan the voluntary submission of the whole people to the trimming of their minds and clipping of their freedom by their government, which through various educational agencies regulates their thoughts, manufactures their feelings, becomes suspiciously watchful when they show signs of inclining towards the spiritual, leading them through a narrow path not towards what is true but what is necessary for the complete welding of them into one uniform mass according to its own recipe. The people accept this all-pervading mental slavery with cheerfulness and pride because of their nervous desire to turn themselves into a machine of power, called the Nation, and emulate other machines in their collective worldliness.

When questioned as to the wisdom of its course, the newly converted fanatic of nationalism answers that 'so long as nations are rampant in this world we have not the option freely to develop our higher humanity. We must utilise every faculty that we possess to resist the evil by assuming it ourselves in the fullest degree. For the only brotherhood possible in the modern world is the brotherhood of hooliganism.' The recognition of the fraternal bond of love between Japan and Russia, which has lately been celebrated with an immense display of rejoicing in Japan, was not owing to any sudden recrudescence of the spirit of Christianity or of Buddhism, but it was a bond established according to the modern faith in a surer relationship of mutual menace of bloodshedding. Yes, one cannot but acknowledge that these facts are the facts of the world of the Nation, and the only moral of it is that all the peoples of the earth should strain their physical, moral and intellectual resources to the utmost to defeat one another in the wrestling match of powerfulness. In ancient days Sparta paid all her attention to becoming powerful; she did become so by crippling her humanity, and died of the amputation.

But it is no consolation to us to know that the weakening of humanity from which the present age is suffering is not limited to the subject races, and that its ravages are even more radical because insidious and voluntary in peoples who are hypnotised into believing that they are free. This bartering of your higher aspirations of life for profit and power has been your own free choice, and I leave you there, at the wreckage of your soul, contemplating your protuberant prosperity. But will you never be called to answer for organising the instincts of self-aggrandisement of whole peoples into perfection and calling it good? I ask you: what disaster has there ever been in the history of man, in its darkest period, like this terrible disaster of the Nation fixing its fangs deep into the naked flesh of the world, taking permanent precautions against its natural relaxation?

You, the people of the West, who have manufactured this abnormality, can you imagine the desolating despair of this haunted world of suffering man possessed by the ghastly abstraction of the organising man? Can you put yourself into the position of the peoples, who seem to have been doomed to an eternal damnation of their own humanity, who not only must suffer continual curtailment of their manhood, but even raise their voices in paeans of praise for the benignity of a mechanical apparatus in its interminable parody of providence?

Have you not seen, since the commencement of the existence of the Nation, that the dread of it has been the one goblin-dread with which the whole world has been trembling? Wherever there is a dark corner, there is the suspicion of its secret malevolence; and people live in a perpetual distrust of their back where they have no eyes. Every sound of a footstep, every rustle of movement in the neighbourhood, sends a thrill of terror all around. And this terror is the parent of all that is base in man's nature. It makes one almost openly unashamed of inhumanity. Clever lies become matters of self-congratulation. Solemn pledges become a farce – laughable for their very solemnity.

The Nation, with all its paraphernalia of power and
prosperity, its flags and pious hymns, its blasphemous
prayers in the churches, and the literary mock thunders
of its patriotic bragging, cannot hide the fact that the
Nation is the greatest evil for the Nation, that all its
precautions are against it, and any new birth of its
fellow in the world is always followed in its mind by
the dread of a new peril. Its one wish is to trade on the
feebleness of the rest of the world, like some insects
that are bred in the paralysed flesh of victims kept just
enough alive to make them toothsome and nutritious.
Therefore it is ready to send its poisonous fluid into
the vitals of the other living peoples who, not being
nations, are harmless. For this the Nation has had
and still has its richest pasture in Asia. Great China,
rich with her ancient wisdom and social ethics, her
discipline of industry and self-control, is like a whale
awakening the lust of spoil in the heart of the Nation.
She is already carrying in her quivering flesh harpoons
sent by the unerring aim of the Nation, the creature of
science and selfishness. Her pitiful attempt to shake
off her traditions of humanity, her social ideals, and
spend her last exhausted resources in drilling herself
into modern efficiency, is thwarted at every step by
the Nation. It is tightening its financial ropes round
her, trying to drag her up on the shore and cut her
into pieces, and then go and offer public thanksgiving
to God for supporting the one existing evil and shattering the possibility of a new one. And for all this
the Nation has been claiming the gratitude of history
and all eternity for its exploitation, ordering its band
of praise to be struck up from end to end of the world,
declaring itself to be the salt of the earth, the flower of
humanity, the blessing of God hurled with all His force
upon the naked skulls of the world of No-Nations.

I know what your advice will be. You will say: form

yourselves into a nation, and resist this encroachment of the Nation. But is this the true advice, that of a man to a man? Why should this be a necessity? I could well believe you if you had said: be more good, more just, more true in your relation to man; control your greed, make your life wholesome in its simplicity and let your consciousness of the divine in humanity be more perfect in its expression. But must you say that it is not the soul, but the machine, which is of the utmost value to ourselves, and that man's salvation depends upon his disciplining himself into a perfection of the dead rhythm of wheels and counterwheels, that machine must be pitted against machine, and nation against nation, in an endless bull-fight of politics?

You say: these machines will come into an agreement for their mutual protection, based upon a conspiracy of fear. But will this federation of steam-boilers supply you with a soul, a soul which has her conscience and her God? What is to happen to that larger part of the world where fear will have no hand in restraining you? Whatever safety they now enjoy, those countries of No-Nation, from the unbridled licence of forge and hammer and turn-screw, results from the mutual jealousy of the powers. But when, instead of being numerous separate machines they become riveted into one organised gregariousness of gluttony, commercial and political, what remotest chance of hope will remain for those others, who have lived and suffered, have loved and worshipped, have thought deeply and worked with meekness, but whose only crime has been that they have not organised?

But, you say, 'That does not matter, the unfit must go to the wall – they shall die, and this is science.'

No, for the sake of your own salvation, I say, they shall *live*, and this is truth. It is extremely bold of me to say so, but I assert that man's world is a moral world, not because we blindly agree to believe it, but because it is so in truth which would be dangerous for us to ignore. And this moral nature of man cannot be divided into convenient compartments for its preservation. You cannot secure it for your home consumption with protective tariff walls, while in foreign parts making it enormously accommodating in its free trade of licence.

Has not this truth already come home to you now, when this cruel war has driven its claws into the vitals of Europe, when her hoard of wealth is bursting into smoke and her humanity is shattered into bits on her battlefields? You ask in amazement: what has she done to deserve this? The answer is that the West has been systematically petrifying her moral nature in order to lay a solid foundation for her gigantic abstractions of efficiency. She has all along been starving the life of the personal man into that of the professional.

In your mediaeval age in Europe, the simple and the natural man, with all his violent passions and desires, was engaged in trying to find out a reconciliation in the conflict between the flesh and the spirit. All through the turbulent career of her vigorous youth the temporal and the spiritual forces both acted strongly upon her nature, and were moulding it into completeness of moral personality. Europe owes all her greatness in humanity to that period of discipline – the discipline of the man in his human integrity.

Then came the age of intellect, of science. We all know that intellect is impersonal. Our life and our heart are one with us, but our mind can be detached from the personal man and then only can it freely move in its world of thoughts. Our intellect is an ascetic who wears no clothes, takes no food, knows no sleep, has no wishes, feels no love or hatred or pity for human limitations, who only reasons unmoved through the vicissitudes of life. It burrows to the roots of things, because it has no personal concern with the thing itself. The grammarian walks straight through all poetry and goes to the root of words without obstruction, because he is seeking not reality, but law. When he finds the law, he is able to teach people how to master words. This is a power – the power which fulfils some special usefulness, some particular need of man.

Reality is the harmony which gives to the component parts of a thing the equilibrium of the whole. You break it, and have in your hands the nomadic atoms fighting against one another, therefore unmeaning. Those who covet power try to get mastery of these aboriginal fighting elements, and through some narrow channels force them into some violent service for some particular needs of man.

This satisfaction of man's needs is a great thing. It gives him freedom in the material world. It confers on him the benefit of a greater range of time and space. He can do things in a shorter time and occupies a larger space with more thoroughness of advantage. Therefore he can easily outstrip those who live in a world of a slower time and of space less fully occupied.

This progress of power attains more and more rapidity of pace. And, for the reason that it is a detached part of man, it soon outruns the complete humanity. The moral man remains behind, because it has to deal with the whole reality, not merely with the law of things, which is impersonal and therefore abstract.

Thus man, with his mental and material power far outgrowing his moral strength, is like an exaggerated giraffe whose head has suddenly shot up miles away from the rest of him, making normal communication difficult to establish. This greedy head, with its huge dental organisation, has been munching all the topmost foliage of the world, but the nourishment is too late in reaching his digestive organs, and his heart is suffering from want of blood. Of this present disharmony in man's nature the West seems to have been blissfully unconscious. The enormity of its material success has diverted all its attention towards self-congratulation on its bulk. The optimism of its logic goes on basing the calculations of its good fortune upon the indefinite prolongation of its railway lines towards eternity. It is superficial enough to think that all tomorrows are merely todays, with the repeated additions of twenty-four hours. It has no fear of the chasm, which is opening wider every day, between man's ever growing storehouses and the emptiness of his hungry humanity. Logic does not know that, under the lowest bed of endless strata of wealth and comforts, earthquakes are being hatched to restore the balance of the moral world; and one day the gaping gulf of spiritual vacuity will draw into its bottom the store of things that have their eternal love for the dust.

Man in his fulness is not powerful, but perfect. Therefore, to turn him into mere power, you have to curtail his soul as much as possible. When we are fully human, we cannot fly at one another's throats; our instincts of social life, our traditions of moral ideals stand in the way. If you want me to take to butchering human beings, you must break up that wholeness of my humanity through some discipline which makes my will dead, my thoughts numb, my movements automatic, and then from the dissolution of the complex personal man will come out that abstraction, that destructive force, which has no relation to human truth, and therefore can be easily brutal or mechanical. Take away man from his natural surroundings, from the fulness of his communal life, with all its living associations of beauty and love and social obligations, and you will be able to turn him into so many fragments of a machine for the production of wealth on a gigantic scale. Turn a tree into a log and it will burn for you, but it will never bear living flowers and fruit.

This process of dehumanising has been going on in commerce and politics. And out of the long birth-throes of mechanical energy has been born this fully developed apparatus of magnificent power and surprising appetite which has been christened in the West as the Nation. As I have hinted before, because of its quality of abstraction it has, with the greatest ease, gone far ahead of the complete moral man. And having the conscience of a ghost and the callous perfection of an automaton, it is causing disasters with which the volcanic dissipations of the youthful moon would be ashamed to be brought into comparison. As a result, the suspicion of man for man stings all the limbs of this civilisation like the hairs of the nettle. Each country is casting its net of espionage into the slimy bottom of the others, fishing for their secrets, the treacherous secrets which brew in the oozy depths of diplomacy. And what is their secret service but the nation's underground trade in kidnapping, murder and treachery and all the ugly crimes bred in the depth of rottenness? Because each nation has its own history of thieving and lies and broken faith, therefore there can only flourish international suspicion and jealousy, and international moral shame becomes anaemic to a degree of ludicrousness. The nation's bagpipe of righteous indignation has so changed its tune according to the variation of time and to the altered groupings of the alliances of diplomacy, that it can be enjoyed with amusement as the variety performance of the political music hall.

I am just coming from my visit to Japan, where

I exhorted this young nation to take its stand upon
the higher ideals of humanity and never to follow the
West in its acceptance of the organised selfishness of
Nationalism as its religion, never to gloat upon the
feebleness of its neighbours, never to be unscrupulous
in its behaviour to the weak, where it can be gloriously
mean with impunity, while turning its right cheek of
brighter humanity for the kiss of admiration to those
who have the power to deal it a blow. Some of the
newspapers praised my utterances for their poetical
qualities, while adding with a leer that it was the
poetry of a defeated people. I felt they were right.
Japan had been taught in a modern school the lesson
how to become powerful. The schooling is done and
she must enjoy the fruits of her lessons. The West in
the voice of her thundering cannon had said at the
door of Japan: let there be a nation – and there was a
Nation. And now that it *has* come into existence, why
do you not feel in your heart of hearts a pure feeling
of gladness and say that it is good? Why is it that I
saw in an English paper an expression of bitterness at
Japan's boasting of her superiority of civilisation – the
thing that the British, along with other nations, have
been carrying on for ages without blushing? Because
the idealism of selfishness must keep itself drunk with
a continual dose of self-laudation. But the same vices
which seem so natural and innocuous in its own life
make it surprised and angry at their unpleasantness
when seen in other nations. Therefore, when you see
the Japanese nation, created in your own image,
launched in its career of national boastfulness, you
shake your head and say, it is not good. Has it not
been one of the causes that raise the cry on these shores
for preparedness to meet one more power of evil with a
greater power of injury? Japan protests that she has her
bushido, that she can never be treacherous to America to

whom she owes her gratitude. But you find it difficult to believe her – for the wisdom of the Nation is not in its faith in humanity but in its complete distrust. You say to yourself that it is not with Japan of the *bushido*, the Japan of the moral ideals, that you have to deal – it is with the abstraction of the popular selfishness, it is with the Nation; and Nation can only trust Nation where their interests coalesce, or at least do not conflict. In fact your instinct tells you that the advent of another people into the arena of nationality makes another addition to the evil which contradicts all that is highest in Man and proves by its success that unscrupulousness is the way to prosperity – and goodness is good for the weak and God is the only remaining consolation of the defeated.

Yes, this is the logic of the Nation. And it will never heed the voice of truth and goodness. It will go on its ring-dance of moral corruption, linking steel unto steel, and machine unto machine, trampling under its tread all the sweet flowers of simple faith and the living ideals of man.

But we delude ourselves into thinking that humanity in these modern days is more to the front than ever before. The reason for this self-delusion is because man is served with the necessaries of life in greater profusion and his physical ills are being alleviated with more efficacy. But the chief part of this is done, not by moral sacrifice, but by intellectual power. In quantity it is great, but it springs from the surface and spreads over the surface. Knowledge and efficiency are powerful in their outward effect, but they are the servants of man, not the man himself. Their service is like the service in a hotel, where it is elaborate, but the host is absent; it is more convenient than hospitable.

Therefore we must not forget that the scientific organisations vastly spreading in all directions are strengthening our power, but not our humanity. With the growth of power the cult of the self-worship of the Nation grows in ascendancy, and the individual willingly allows the Nation to take donkey-rides upon his back; and there happens the anomaly which must have such disastrous effects, that the individual worships with all sacrifices a god which is morally much inferior to himself. This could never have been possible if the god had been as real as the individual.

Let me give an illustration of this point. In some parts of India it has been enjoined as an act of great piety for a widow to go without food and water on a particular day every fortnight. This often leads to cruelty, unmeaning and inhuman. And yet men are not by nature cruel to such a degree. But this piety being a mere unreal abstraction completely deadens the moral sense of the individual, just as the man who would not hurt an animal unnecessarily would cause horrible suffering to a large number of innocent creatures when he drugs his feelings with the abstract idea of 'sport'! Because these ideas are creations of our intellect, because they are logical classifications, therefore they can so easily hide in their mist the personal man.

And the idea of the Nation is one of the most powerful anaesthetics that man has invented. Under the influence of its fumes the whole people can carry out its systematic programme of the most virulent self-seeking without being in the least aware of its moral perversion – in fact can feel dangerously resentful if it is pointed out.

But can this go on indefinitely, continually producing barrenness of moral insensibility upon a large tract of our living nature? Can it escape its nemesis for ever? Has this giant power of mechanical organisation no limit in this world against which it may shatter itself all the more completely because of its terrible strength and velocity? Do you believe that evil can be permanently kept in check by competition with evil, and that conference of prudence can keep the devil chained in its makeshift cage of mutual agreement?

This European war of Nations is the war of retribution. Man, the person, must protest for his very life against the heaping up of things where there should be the heart, and systems and policies where there should flow living human relationship. The time has come when, for the sake of the whole outraged world, Europe should fully know in her own person the terrible absurdity of the thing called the Nation.

The Nation has thriven long upon mutilated humanity. Men, the fairest creations of God, came out of the National manufactory in huge numbers as war-making and money-making puppets, ludicrously vain of their pitiful perfection of mechanism. Human society grew more and more into a marionette show of politicians, soldiers, manufacturers and bureaucrats, pulled by wire arrangements of wonderful efficiency.

But the apotheosis of selfishness can never make its interminable breed of hatred and greed, fear and hypocrisy, suspicion and tyranny, an end in themselves. These monsters grow into huge shapes but never into harmony. And this Nation may grow on to an unimaginable corpulence, not of a living body, but of steel and steam and office buildings, till its deformity can contain no longer its ugly voluminousness – till it begins to crack and gape, breathe gas and fire in gasps, and its death-rattles sound in cannon roars. In this war the death-throes of the Nation have commenced. Suddenly, all its mechanism going mad, it has begun the dance of the Furies, shattering its own limbs, scattering them into the dust. It is the fifth act of the tragedy of the unreal.

Those who have any faith in Man cannot but fervently hope that the tyranny of the Nation will not be restored to all its former teeth and claws, to its far-reaching iron arms and its immense inner cavity, all stomach and no heart; that man will have his new birth, in the freedom of his individuality, from the enveloping vagueness of abstraction.

The veil has been raised, and in this frightful war the West has stood face to face with her own creation, to which she had offered her soul. She must know what it truly is.

She had never let herself suspect what slow decay and decomposition were secretly going on in her moral nature, which often broke out in doctrines of scepticism, but still oftener and in still more dangerously subtle manner showed itself in her unconsciousness of the mutilation and insult that she had been inflicting upon a vast part of the world. Now she must know the truth nearer home.

And then there will come from her own children those who will break themselves free from the slavery of this illusion, this perversion of brotherhood founded upon self-seeking, those who will own themselves as God's children and as no bond-slaves of machinery, which turns souls into commodities and life into compartments, which, with its iron claws, scratches out the heart of the world and knows not what it has done.

And we of the no nations of the world, whose heads have been bowed to the dust, will know that this dust is more sacred than the bricks which build the pride of power. For this dust is fertile of life, and of beauty and worship. We shall thank God that we were made to wait in silence through the night of despair, had to bear the insult of the proud and the strong man's burden, yet all through it, though our hearts quaked with doubt and fear, never could we blindly believe in the salvation which machinery offered to man, but we held fast to our trust in God and the truth of the human soul. And we can still cherish the hope that, when power becomes ashamed to occupy its throne and is ready to make way for love, when the morning comes for cleansing the blood-stained steps of the Nation along the highroad of humanity, we shall be called upon to bring our own vessel of sacred water – the water of worship – to sweeten the history of man into purity, and with its sprinkling make the trampled dust of the centuries blessed with fruitfulness.

Nationalism in India

Our real problem in India is not political. It is
social. This is a condition not only prevailing in
India, but among all nations. I do not believe in
an exclusive political interest. Politics in the West
have dominated western ideals, and we in India are
trying to imitate you. We have to remember that in
Europe, where peoples had their racial unity from the
beginning, and where natural resources were insufficient for the inhabitants, the civilisation has naturally
taken on the character of political and commercial
aggressiveness. For on the one hand they had no
internal complications, and on the other they had to
deal with neighbours who were strong and rapacious.
To have perfect combination among themselves and a
watchful attitude of animosity against others was taken
as the solution of their problems. In former days they
organised and plundered; in the present age the same
spirit continues – and they organise and exploit the
whole world.

But from the earliest beginnings of history India
has had her own problem constantly before her – it
is the race problem. Each nation must be conscious of

its mission, and we in India must realise that we cut a poor figure when we try to be political, simply because we have not yet been finally able to accomplish what was set before us by our providence.

This problem of race unity which we have been trying to solve for so many years has likewise to be faced by you here in America. Many people in this country ask me what is happening to the caste distinctions in India. But when this question is asked me, it is usually done with a superior air. And I feel tempted to put the same question to our American critics with a slight modification: 'What have you done with the Red Indian and the Negro?' For you have not got over your attitude of caste towards them. You have used violent methods to keep aloof from other races, but until you have solved the question, here in America, you have no right to question India.

In spite of our great difficulty, however, India has done something. She has tried to make an adjustment of races, to acknowledge the real differences between them where these exist, and yet seek for some basis of unity. This basis has come through our saints, like Nanak, Kabir, Chaitanya* and others, preaching one God to all races of India.

In finding the solution of our problem we shall have helped to solve the world problem as well. What India has been, the whole world is now. The whole world is becoming one country through scientific facility. And the moment is arriving when you must also find a basis of unity which is not political. If India can offer to the world her solution, it will be a contribution to humanity. There is only one history – the history of man. All national histories are merely chapters in the larger one. And we are content in India to suffer for such a great cause.

* Nanak (1469-1533), Kabir (1440-1518), Chaitanya (1485-1533).

Each individual has his self-love. Therefore his brute instinct leads him to fight with others in the sole pursuit of his self-interest. But man has also his higher instincts of sympathy and mutual help. The people who are lacking in this higher moral power and who therefore cannot combine in fellowship with one another must perish or live in a state of degradation. Only those peoples have survived and achieved civilisation who have this spirit of co-operation strong in them. So we find that from the beginning of history men had to choose between fighting with one another and combining, between serving their own interest or the common interest of all.

In our early history, when the geographical limits of each country and also the facilities of communication were small, this problem was comparatively small in dimension. It was sufficient for men to develop their sense of unity within their area of segregation. In those days they combined among themselves and fought against others. But it was this moral spirit of combination which was the true basis of their greatness, and this fostered their art, science and religion. At that early time the most important fact that man had to take count of was the fact of the members of one particular race of men coming in close contact with one another. Those who truly grasped this fact through their higher nature made their mark in history.

The most important fact of the present age is that all the different races of men have come close together. And again we are confronted with two alternatives. The problem is whether the different groups of peoples shall go on fighting with one another or find out some true basis of reconciliation and mutual help; whether it will be interminable competition or co-operation.

I have no hesitation in saying that those who

are gifted with the moral power of love and vision of
spiritual unity, who have the least feeling of enmity
against aliens, and the sympathetic insight to place
themselves in the position of others, will be the fittest
to take their permanent place in the age that is lying
before us, and those who are constantly developing
their instincts for fight and intolerance of aliens will
be eliminated. For this is the problem before us, and we
have to prove our humanity by solving it through the
help of our higher nature. The gigantic organisations
for hurting others and warding off their blows, for
making money by dragging others back, will not help
us. On the contrary, by their crushing weight, their
enormous cost and their deadening effect upon living
humanity, they will seriously impede our freedom in
the larger life of a higher civilisation.

During the evolution of the Nation the moral
culture of brotherhood was limited by geographical
boundaries, because at that time those boundaries
were true. Now they have become imaginary lines
of tradition divested of the qualities of real obstacles.
So the time has come when man's moral nature must
deal with this great fact with all seriousness or perish.
The first impulse of this change of circumstance has
been the churning up of man's baser passions of greed
and cruel hatred. If this persists indefinitely, and armaments go on exaggerating themselves to unimaginable
absurdities, and machines and storehouses envelop
this fair earth with their dirt and smoke and ugliness,
then it will end in a conflagration of suicide. Therefore
man will have to exert all his power of love and clarity
of vision to make another great moral adjustment
which will comprehend the whole world of men and
not merely the fractional groups of nationality. The
call has come to every individual in the present age
to prepare himself and his surroundings for this dawn

of a new era, when man shall discover his soul in the spiritual unity of all human beings.

If it is given at all to the West to struggle out of these tangles of the lower slopes to the spiritual summit of humanity then I cannot but think that it is the special mission of America to fulfil this hope of God and man. You are the country of expectation, desiring something else than what is. Europe has her subtle habits of mind and her conventions. But America, as yet, has come to no conclusions. I realise how much America is untrammelled by the traditions of the past, and I can appreciate that experimentalism is a sign of America's youth. The foundation of her glory is in the future, rather than in the past, and if one is gifted with the power of clairvoyance, one will be able to love the America that is to be.

America is destined to justify western civilisation to the East. Europe has lost faith in humanity, and has become distrustful and sickly. America, on the other hand, is not pessimistic or blasé. You know, as a people, that there is such a thing as a better and a best, and that knowledge drives you on. There are habits that are not merely passive but aggressively arrogant. They are not like mere walls, but are like hedges of stinging nettles. Europe has been cultivating these hedges of habits for long years, till they have grown round her dense and strong and high. The pride of her traditions has sent its roots deep into her heart. I do not wish to contend that it is unreasonable. But pride in every form breeds blindness at the end. Like all artificial stimulants its first effect is a heightening of consciousness, and then with the increasing dosage it muddles it and brings an exultation that is misleading. Europe has gradually grown hardened in her pride in all her outer and inner habits. She not only cannot forget that she is western, but she takes every opportunity to hurl this fact against others to humiliate them. This is why she is growing incapable of imparting to the East what is best in herself, and of accepting in a right spirit the wisdom that the East has stored for centuries.

In America national habits and traditions have not had time to spread their clutching roots round your hearts. You have constantly felt and complained of your disadvantages when you compared your nomadic restlessness with the settled traditions of Europe — the Europe which can show her picture of greatness to the best advantage because she can fix it against the background of the past. But in this present age of transition, when a new era of civilisation is sending its trumpet-call to all peoples of the world across an unlimited future, this very freedom of detachment will enable you to accept its invitation and to achieve the goal for which Europe began her journey but lost herself mid-way. For she was tempted out of her path by her pride of power and greed of possession.

Not merely your freedom from habits of mind in individuals, but also the freedom of your history from all unclean entanglements, fits you in your career of holding the banner of civilisation of the future. All the great nations of Europe have their victims in other parts of the world. This not only deadens their moral sympathy but also their intellectual sympathy, which is so necessary for the understanding of races which are different from one's own. Englishmen can never truly understand India, because their minds are not disinterested with regard to that country. If you compare England with Germany or France you will find she has produced the smallest number of scholars who have studied Indian literature and philosophy with any amount of sympathetic insight or thoroughness. This attitude of apathy and contempt is natural where the relationship is abnormal and founded upon national selfishness and pride. But your history has been disinterested, and that is why you have been able to help Japan in her lessons in western civilisation, and that is why China can look upon you with the best confidence in this, her darkest period of danger. In fact you are carrying all the responsibility of a great future because you are untrammelled by the grasping miserliness of a past. Therefore, of all countries of the earth, America has to be fully conscious of this future; her vision must not be obscured and her faith in humanity must be strong with the strength of youth.

A parallelism exists between America and India – the parallelism of welding together into one body various races.

In my country we have been seeking to find out something common to all races, which will prove their real unity. No nation looking for a mere political or commercial basis of unity will find such a solution sufficient. Men of thought and power will discover the spiritual unity, will realise it, and preach it.

India has never had a real sense of nationalism. Even though from childhood I had been taught that idolatry of the Nation is almost better than reverence for God and humanity, I believe I have outgrown that teaching, and it is my conviction that my countrymen will truly gain their India by fighting against the education which teaches them that a country is greater than the ideals of humanity.

The educated Indian at present is trying to absorb some lessons from history contrary to the lessons of our ancestors. The East, in fact, is attempting to take unto itself a history, which is not the outcome of its own living. Japan, for example, thinks she is getting powerful through adopting western methods but, after she has exhausted her inheritance, only the borrowed weapons of civilisation will remain to her. She will not have developed herself from within.

Europe has her past. Europe's strength therefore lies in her history. We in India must make up our minds that we cannot borrow other people's history, and that if we stifle our own we are committing suicide. When you borrow things that do not belong to your life, they only serve to crush your life.

And therefore I believe that it does India no good to compete with western civilisation in its own field. But we shall be more than compensated if, in spite of the insults heaped upon us, we follow our own destiny.

There are lessons which impart information or train our minds for intellectual pursuits. These are simple and can be acquired and used with advantage. But there are others which affect our deeper nature and change our direction of life. Before we accept them and pay their value by selling our own inheritance, we must pause and think deeply. In man's history there come ages of fireworks which dazzle us by their force and movement. They laugh not only at our modest household lamps but also at the eternal stars. But let us not for that provocation be precipitate in our desire to dismiss our lamps. Let us patiently bear our present insult and realise that these fireworks have splendour but not permanence, because of the extreme explosiveness which is the cause of their power, and also of their exhaustion. They are spending a fatal quantity of energy and substance compared to their gain and production.

Anyhow, our ideals have been evolved through our own history, and even if we wished we could only make poor fireworks of them because their materials are different from yours, as is also their moral purpose. If we cherish the desire of paying our all to buy a political nationality it will be as absurd as if Switzerland had staked her existence on her ambition to build up a navy powerful enough to compete with that of England. The mistake that we make is in thinking that man's channel of greatness is only one – the one which has made itself painfully evident for the time being by its depth of insolence.

We must know for certain that there is a future before us and that future is waiting for those who are rich in moral ideals and not in mere things. And it is the privilege of man to work for fruits that are beyond his immediate reach, and to adjust his life not in slavish conformity to the examples of some present success or even to his own prudent past, limited in its aspiration, but to an infinite future bearing in its heart the ideals of our highest expectations.

We must recognise that it is providential that the West has come to India. And yet someone must show the East to the West, and convince the West that the East has her contribution to make to the history of civilisation. India is no beggar of the West. And yet even though the West may think she is, I am not for thrusting off western civilisation and becoming segregated in our independence. Let us have a deep association. If Providence wants England to be the channel of that communication, of that deeper association, I am willing to accept it with all humility. I have great faith in human nature, and I think the West will find its true mission. I speak bitterly of western civilisation when I am conscious that it is betraying its trust and thwarting its own purpose. The West must not make herself a curse to the world by using her power for her own selfish needs but, by teaching the ignorant and helping the weak, she should save herself from the worst danger that the strong is liable to incur by making the feeble acquire power enough to resist her intrusion. And also she must not make her materialism to be the final thing, but must realise that she is doing a service in freeing the spiritual being from the tyranny of matter.

I am not against one nation in particular, but against the general idea of all nations. What is the Nation?

It is the aspect of a whole people as an organised power. This organisation incessantly keeps up the insistence of the population on becoming strong and efficient. But this strenuous effort after strength and efficiency drains man's energy from his higher nature where he is self-sacrificing and creative. For thereby man's power of sacrifice is diverted from his ultimate object, which is moral, to the maintenance of this organisation, which is mechanical. Yet in this he feels all the satisfaction of moral exaltation and therefore becomes supremely dangerous to humanity. He feels relieved of the urging of his conscience when he can transfer his responsibility to this machine which is the creation of his intellect and not of his complete moral personality. By this device the people which loves freedom perpetuates slavery in a large portion of the world with the comfortable feeling of pride in having done its duty; men who are naturally just can be cruelly unjust both in their act and their thought, accompanied by a feeling that they are helping the world to receive its deserts; men who are honest can blindly go on robbing others of their human rights for self-aggrandisement, all the while abusing the deprived for not deserving better treatment. We have seen in our everyday life even small organisations of business and profession produce callousness of feeling in men who are not naturally bad, and we can well imagine what a moral havoc it is causing in a world where whole peoples are furiously organising themselves for gaining wealth and power.

Nationalism is a great menace. It is the particular thing which for years has been at the bottom of India's troubles. And inasmuch as we have been ruled and dominated by a nation that is strictly political in its attitude, we have tried to develop within ourselves, despite our inheritance from the past, a belief in our eventual political destiny.

There are different parties in India, with different ideals. Some are struggling for political independence. Others think that the time has not arrived for that, and yet believe that India should have the rights that the English colonies have. They wish to gain autonomy as far as possible.

In the beginning of the history of political agitation in India there was not the conflict between parties which there is today. At that time there was a party known as the Indian Congress;* they had no real programme. They had a few grievances for redress by the authorities. They wanted larger representation in the Council House, and more freedom in Municipal Government. They wanted scraps of things, but they had no constructive ideal. Therefore I was lacking in enthusiasm for their methods. It was my conviction that what India most needed was constructive work coming from within herself. In this work we must take all risks and go on doing the duties which by right are ours, though in the teeth of persecution, winning moral victory at every step, by our failure and suffering. We must show those who are over us that we have in ourselves the strength of moral power, the power to suffer for truth. Where we have nothing to show, we have only to beg. It would be mischievous if the gifts we wish for were granted to us at once, and I have told my countrymen, time and again, to combine for the work of creating opportunities to give vent to

* The Indian National Congress was founded in 1885.

our spirit of self-sacrifice, and not for the purpose of begging.

The party, however, lost power because the people soon came to realise how futile was the half policy adopted by them. The party split,* and there arrived the Extremists, who advocated independence of action, and discarded the begging method – the easiest method of relieving one's mind from his responsibility towards his country. Their ideals were based on western history. They had no sympathy with the special problems of India. They did not recognise the patent fact that there were causes in our social organisation which made the Indian incapable of coping with the alien. What should we do if, for any reason, England was driven away? We should simply be victims for other nations. The same social weaknesses would prevail. The thing we in India have to think of is this: to remove those social customs and ideals which have generated a want of self-respect and a complete dependence on those above us – a state of affairs which has been brought about entirely by the domination in India of the caste system, and the blind and lazy habit of relying upon the authority of traditions that are incongruous anachronisms in the present age.

Once again I draw your attention to the difficulties India has had to encounter and her struggle to overcome them. Her problem was the problem of the world in miniature. India is too vast in its area and too diverse in its races. It is many countries packed in one geographical receptacle. It is just the opposite of what Europe truly is: namely, one country made into many. Thus Europe in its culture and growth has had the advantage of the strength of the many as well as

* In 1907, at the annual session of the Indian National Congress, held at Surat.

the strength of the one. India, on the contrary, being naturally many, yet adventitiously one, has all along suffered from the looseness of its diversity and the feebleness of its unity. A true unity is like a round globe; it rolls on, carrying its burden easily. But diversity is a many-cornered thing which has to be dragged and pushed with all force. Be it said to the credit of India that this diversity was not her own creation; she has had to accept it as a fact from the beginning of her history. In America and Australia, Europe has simplified her problem by almost exterminating the original population. Even in the present age this spirit of extermination is making itself manifest, in the inhospitable shutting out of aliens, by those who themselves were aliens in the lands they now occupy. But India tolerated difference of races from the first, and that spirit of toleration has acted all through her history.

Her caste system is the outcome of this spirit of toleration. For India has all along been trying experiments in evolving a social unity within which all the different peoples could be held together, while fully enjoying the freedom of maintaining their own differences. The tie has been as loose as possible, yet as close as the circumstances permitted. This has produced something like a United States of a social federation, whose common name is Hinduism.

India had felt that diversity of races there must be and should be, whatever may be its drawbacks, and you can never coerce nature into your narrow limits of convenience without paying one day very dearly for it. In this India was right; but what she failed to realise was that in human beings differences are not like the physical barriers of mountains, fixed for ever – they are fluid with life's flow, they are changing their courses and their shapes and volumes.

Therefore in her caste regulations India recognised differences, but not the mutability which is the law of life. In trying to avoid collisions she set up boundaries of immovable walls, thus giving to her numerous races the negative benefit of peace and order but not the positive opportunity of expansion and movement. She accepted nature where it produces diversity, but ignored it where it uses that diversity for its world-game of infinite permutations and combinations. She treated life in all truth where it is manifold, but insulted it where it is ever moving. Therefore Life departed from her social system and in its place she is worshipping with all ceremony the magnificent cage of countless compartments that she has manufactured.

The same thing happened where she tried to ward off the collisions of trade interests. She associated different trades and professions with different castes. This had the effect of allaying for good the interminable jealousy and hatred of competition – the competition which breeds cruelty and makes the atmosphere thick with lies and deception. In this also India laid all her emphasis upon the law of heredity, ignoring the law of mutation, and thus gradually reduced arts into crafts and genius into skill.

However, what western observers fail to discern is that in her caste system India in all seriousness accepted her responsibility to solve the race problem in such a manner as to avoid all friction, and yet to afford each race freedom within its boundaries. Let us admit India has not in this achieved a full measure of success. But this you must also concede: that the West, being more favourably situated as to homogeneity of races, has never given her attention to this problem, and whenever confronted with it she has tried to make it easy by ignoring it altogether. And this is the source of her anti-Asiatic agitations for depriving aliens of their right to earn their honest living on these shores. In most of your colonies you only admit them on condition of their accepting the menial positions of hewers of wood and drawers of water. Either you shut your doors against the aliens or reduce them into slavery. And this is your solution to the problem of race-conflict. Whatever may be its merits you will have to admit that it does not spring from the higher impulses of civilisation, but from the lower passions of greed and hatred. You say this is human nature – and India also thought she knew human nature when she strongly barricaded her race distinctions by the fixed barriers of social gradations. But we have found out to our cost that human nature is not what it seems, but what it is in truth, which is in its infinite possibilities. And when we in our blindness insult humanity for its ragged appearance it sheds its disguise to disclose to us that we have insulted our God. The degradation which we cast upon others in our pride or self-interest degrades our own humanity – and this is the punishment which is most terrible, because we do not detect it till it is too late.

Not only in your relation with aliens but with the different sections of your own society you have not achieved harmony of reconciliation. The spirit of conflict and competition is allowed the full freedom of its reckless career. And because its genesis is the greed of wealth and power it can never come to any other end but to a violent death. In India the production of commodities was brought under the law of social adjustments. Its basis was co-operation, having for its object the perfect satisfaction of social needs. But in the West it is guided by the impulse of competition, whose end is the gain of wealth for individuals. But the individual is like the geometrical line; it is length without breadth. It has not got the depth to be able to hold anything permanently. Therefore its greed or gain can never come to finality. In its lengthening process of growth it can cross other lines and cause entanglements, but will ever go on missing the ideal of completeness in its thinness of isolation.

In all our physical appetites we recognise a limit. We know that to exceed that limit is to exceed the limit of health. But has this lust for wealth and power no bounds beyond which is death's dominion? In these national carnivals of materialism are not the western peoples spending most of their vital energy in merely producing things and neglecting the creation of ideals? And can a civilisation ignore the law of moral health and go on in its endless process of inflation by gorging upon material things? Man in his social ideals naturally tries to regulate his appetites, subordinating them to the higher purpose of his nature. But in the economic world our appetites follow no other restrictions but those of supply and demand which can be artificially fostered, affording individuals opportunities for indulgence in an endless feast of grossness. In India our social instincts imposed restrictions upon our appetites – maybe it went to the extreme of repression – but in the West the spirit of economic organisation with no moral purpose goads the people into the perpetual pursuit of wealth; but has this no wholesome limit?

The ideals that strive to take form in social institutions have two objects. One is to regulate our passions and appetites for the harmonious development of man, and the other is to help him to cultivate disinterested love for his fellow-creatures. Therefore society is the expression of those moral and spiritual aspirations of man which belong to his higher nature.

Our food is creative, it builds our body; but not so wine, which stimulates. Our social ideals create the human world, but when our mind is diverted from them to greed of power then in that state of intoxication we live in a world of abnormality where our strength is not health and our liberty is not freedom. Therefore political freedom does not give us freedom when our mind is not free. An automobile does not create freedom of movement, because it is a mere machine. When I myself am free I can use the automobile for the purpose of my freedom.

We must never forget in the present day that those people who have got their political freedom are not necessarily free; they are merely powerful. The passions which are unbridled in them are creating huge organisations of slavery in the disguise of freedom. Those who have made the gain of money their highest end are unconsciously selling their life and soul to rich persons or to the combinations that represent money. Those who are enamoured of their political power and gloat over their extension of dominion over foreign races gradually surrender their own freedom and humanity to the organisations necessary for holding other peoples in slavery. In the so-called free countries the majority of the people are not free; they are driven by the minority to a goal which is not even known to them. This becomes possible only because people do not acknowledge moral and spiritual freedom as their object. They create huge eddies with their passions, and they feel dizzily inebriated with the mere velocity of their whirling movement, taking that to be freedom. But the doom which is waiting to overtake them is as certain as death – for man's truth is moral truth and his emancipation is in the spiritual life.

The general opinion of the majority of the present-day nationalists in India is that we have come to a final completeness in our social and spiritual ideals, the task of the constructive work of society having been done several thousand years before we were born, and that now we are free to employ all our activities in the political direction. We never dream of blaming our social inadequacy as the origin of our present helplessness, for we have accepted as the creed of our nationalism that this social system has been perfected for all time to come by our ancestors, who had the superhuman vision of all eternity and supernatural power for making infinite provision for future ages. Therefore, for all our miseries and shortcomings, we hold responsible the historical surprises that burst upon us from outside. This is the reason why we think that our one task is to build a political miracle of freedom upon the quicksand of social slavery. In fact we want to dam up the true course of our own historical stream, and only borrow power from the sources of other peoples' history.

Those of us in India who have come under the delusion that mere political freedom will make us free have accepted their lessons from the West as the gospel truth and lost their faith in humanity. We must remember that whatever weakness we cherish in our society will become the source of danger in politics. The same inertia which leads us to our idolatry of dead forms in social institutions will create in our politics prison-houses with immovable walls. The narrowness of sympathy which makes it possible for us to impose upon a considerable portion of humanity the galling yoke of inferiority will assert itself in our politics in creating the tyranny of injustice.

When our nationalists talk about ideals they forget that the basis of nationalism is wanting. The very people who are upholding these ideals are themselves the most conservative in their social practice. Nationalists say, for example: look at Switzerland where, in spite of race differences, the people have solidified into a nation. Yet, remember that in Switzerland the races can mingle, they can intermarry, because they are of the same blood. In India there is no common birthright. And when we talk of western nationality we forget that the nations there do not have that physical repulsion, one for the other, that we have between different castes. Have we an instance in the whole world where a people who are not allowed to mingle their blood shed their blood for one another except by coercion or for mercenary purposes? And can we ever hope that these moral barriers against our race amalgamation will not stand in the way of our political unity?

Then again we must give full recognition to this fact that our social restrictions are still tyrannical, so much so as to make men cowards. If a man tells me that he has heterodox ideas, but that he cannot follow them because he would be socially ostracised, I excuse him for having to live a life of untruth, in order to live at all. The social habit of mind which impels us to make the life of our fellow-beings a burden to them where they differ from us even in such a thing as their choice of food, is sure to persist in our political organisation and result in creating engines of coercion to crush every rational difference which is the sign of life. And tyranny will only add to the inevitable lies and hypocrisy in our political life. Is the mere name of freedom so valuable that we should be willing to sacrifice for its sake our moral freedom?

The intemperance of our habits does not immediately show its effects when we are in the vigour of our youth. But it gradually consumes that vigour, and when the period of decline sets in then we have to settle accounts and pay off our debts, which leads us to insolvency. In the West you are still able to carry your head high, though your humanity is suffering every moment from its dipsomania of organising power. India also in the heyday of her youth could carry in her vital organs the dead weight of her social organisations stiffened to rigid perfection, but it has been fatal to her, and has produced a gradual paralysis of her living nature. And this is the reason why the educated community of India has become insensible of her social needs. They are taking the very immobility of our social structures as the sign of their perfection – and because the healthy feeling of pain is dead in the limbs of our social organism they delude themselves into thinking that it needs no ministration. Therefore they think that all their energies need their only scope in the political field. It is like a man whose legs have become shrivelled and useless, trying to delude himself that these limbs have grown still because they have attained their ultimate salvation, and all that is wrong about him is the shortness of his sticks.

So much for the social and the political regeneration of India. Now we come to her industries, and I am very often asked whether there is in India any industrial regeneration since the advent of the British government. It must be remembered that at the beginning of the British rule in India our industries were suppressed, and since then we have not met with any real help or encouragement to enable us to make a stand against the monster commercial organisations of the world. The nations have decreed that we must remain purely an agricultural people, even forgetting the use of arms for all time to come. Thus India is being turned into so many predigested morsels of food ready to be swallowed at any moment by any nation which has even the most rudimentary set of teeth in its head.

India therefore has very little outlet for her industrial originality. I personally do not believe in the unwieldy organisations of the present day. The very fact that they are ugly shows that they are in discordance with the whole creation. The vast powers of nature do not reveal their truth in hideousness, but in beauty. Beauty is the signature which the Creator stamps upon His works when He is satisfied with them. All our products that insolently ignore the laws of perfection and are unashamed in their display of ungainliness bear the perpetual weight of God's displeasure. So far as your commerce lacks the dignity of grace it is untrue. Beauty and her twin brother Truth require leisure and self-control for their growth. But the greed of gain has no time or limit to its capaciousness. Its one object is to produce and consume. It has pity neither for beautiful nature nor for living human beings. It is ruthlessly ready without a moment's hesitation to crush beauty and life out of them, moulding them into money. It is this ugly vulgarity of commerce which brought upon it the censure of contempt in our earlier days, when men had leisure to have an unclouded vision of perfection in humanity. Men in those times were rightly ashamed of the instinct of mere money-making. But in this scientific age money, by its very abnormal bulk, has won its throne. And when from its eminence of piled-up things it insults the higher instincts of man, banishing beauty and noble sentiments from its surroundings, we submit. For we in our meanness have accepted bribes from its hands and our imagination has grovelled in the dust before its immensity of flesh.

But its very unwieldiness and its endless complexities are its true signs of failure. The swimmer who is an expert does not exhibit his muscular force by violent movements, but exhibits some power which is invisible and which shows itself in perfect grace and reposefulness. The true distinction of man from animals is in his power and worth which are inner

and invisible. But the present-day commercial civilisation of man is not only taking too much time and
space but killing time and space. Its movements are
violent; its noise is discordantly loud. It is carrying its
own damnation because it is trampling into distortion
the humanity upon which it stands. It is strenuously
turning out money at the cost of happiness. Man is
reducing himself to his minimum in order to be able
to make amplest room for his organisations. He is
deriding his human sentiments into shame because
they are apt to stand in the way of his machines.

In our mythology we have the legend that the man
who performs penances for attaining immortality has
to meet with temptations sent by Indra, the Lord of
the Immortals. If he is lured by them he is lost. The
West has been striving for centuries after its goal of
immortality. Indra has sent her the temptation to try
her. It is the gorgeous temptation of wealth. She has
accepted it, and her civilisation of humanity has lost
its path in the wilderness of machinery.

This commercialism with its barbarity of ugly
decorations is a terrible menace to all humanity,
because it is setting up the ideal of power over that of
perfection. It is making the cult of self-seeking exult in
its naked shamelessness. Our nerves are more delicate
than our muscles. Things that are the most precious
in us are helpless as babes when we take away from
them the careful protection which they claim from
us for their very preciousness. Therefore, when the
callous rudeness of power runs amuck in the broad-
way of humanity it scares away by its grossness the
ideals which we have cherished with the martyrdom
of centuries.

The temptation which is fatal for the strong is still
more so for the weak. And I do not welcome it in our
Indian life, even though it be sent by the Lord of the

Immortals. Let our life be simple in its outer aspect and rich in its inner gain. Let our civilisation take its firm stand upon its basis of social co-operation and not upon that of economic exploitation and conflict. How to do it in the teeth of the drainage of our life-blood by the economic dragons is the task set before the thinkers of all oriental nations who have faith in the human soul. It is a sign of laziness and impotency to accept conditions imposed upon us by others who have other ideals than ours. We should actively try to adapt the world powers to guide our history to its own perfect end.

From the above you will know that I am not an economist. I am willing to acknowledge that there is a law of demand and supply and an infatuation of man for more things than are good for him. And yet I will persist in believing that there is such a thing as the harmony of completeness in humanity, where poverty does not take away his riches, where defeat may lead him to victory, death to immortality, and where in the compensation of Eternal Justice those who are the last may yet have their insult transmuted into a golden triumph.

Appendix

Tagore's Visit to the United States: 1916–17

Tagore arrived in Seattle from Japan on 18 September 1916. The following schedule shows his formal speaking engagements as well as some of the other occasions on which he spoke less formally and/or gave readings from his work.

25 Sept.	Seattle, Washington: lectured twice on 'The Cult of Nationalism'.
26 Sept.	Portland, Oregon: lectured on 'Nationalism'.
2 Oct.	San Francisco, California: lectured on 'Nationalism'.
6 Oct.	Santa Barbara, California: lectured on 'Nationalism'.
9 Oct.	Los Angeles, California: lectured on 'The Cult of Nationalism'.
10 Oct.	Pasadena, California: spoke on 'Nationalism'.

14 Oct.	Salt Lake City, Utah: lectured on 'Nationalism'.
16 Oct.	Denver, Colorado: lectured on 'Nationalism'.
20 Oct.	Chicago, Illinois: lectured on 'The Cult of Nationalism'.
30 Oct.	Indianapolis, Indiana: spoke on 'Nationalism'. (Also visited Ames, Iowa.)
4 Nov.	Milwaukee, Wisconsin: spoke on 'Nationalism'.
6 Nov.	Louisville, Kentucky: spoke on 'The World of Personality'.
8 Nov.	Nashville, Tennessee: spoke on 'Nationalism'.
9 Nov.	(Cincinnati, Ohio.)
10 Nov.	Detroit, Michigan: spoke on 'Nationalism'.
14 Nov.	Cleveland, Ohio: spoke on 'The World of Personality'.
21 Nov.	New York City: lectured on 'The Cult of Nationalism'.
23 Nov.	New York City: lectured on 'The World of Personality'.
26 Nov. (?)	New York City: spoke on 'Nationalism'.
28 Nov.	Paterson, New Jersey: spoke on 'Nationalism'.
29 Nov.	Philadelphia, Pennsylvania: lectured on 'The Cult of Nationalism'.

4 Dec.	Boston, Massachusetts: spoke on 'What is Art?'
5 Dec.	Boston, Massachusetts: lectured on 'The Cult of Nationalism'.
6 Dec.	(New Haven, Connecticut.)
7 Dec.	Northampton, New York: spoke on 'Shantiniketan'.
8–12 Dec. (?)	(New York City.)
13 Dec.	Pittsburgh, Pennsylvania: lectured on 'The Cult of Nationalism'.
16 Dec.	Cleveland, Ohio: lectured on 'The Cult of Nationalism'.
17–22 Dec.	(Chicago.)
24–31 Dec.	Urbana, Illinois: spoke on 'Personality in Art' (24 Dec.), 'The World of Personality' (25 Dec.), 'The Second Birth' (26 Dec.), 'Shantiniketan' (28 Dec.), 'Nationalism in the West' (29 Dec.), 'Nationalism in India' (30 Dec.).
1–7 Jan. (?)	(Chicago.)
8 Jan.	Lincoln, Nebraska: spoke on 'Nationalism'.
9 Jan.	Des Moines, Iowa: spoke on 'Nationalism'.
10 Jan.	Omaha, Nebraska: spoke on 'Nationalism'.

Tagore travelled back via Colorado Springs and left for Japan from San Francisco on 21 January 1917.

Select Bibliography

Elmhirst, Leonard K., *Poet and Plowman*, Calcutta, Vishva Bharati, 1975

Hay, Stephen N., *Asian Ideas of East and West: Tagore and his critics in Japan, China and India*, Harvard University Press, 1970

Kripalani, Krishna, *Rabindranath Tagore: A Biography*, London, Oxford University Press, 1962 (2nd edn, Calcutta, Vishva Bharati, 1980)

Mukherjee, Sujit, *Passage to America: The Reception of Rabindranath Tagore in the United States, 1912-1941*, Calcutta, Bookland, 1964

Tagore, Rabindranath,

Creative Unity, London, Macmillan, 1922

Gitanjali, London, Macmillan, 1913

Glimpses of Bengal, London, Macmillan, 1921 (2nd edn, 1991)

The Home and the World, London, Macmillan, 1919 (2nd edn, Penguin, 1985)

My Reminiscences, London, Macmillan, 1917 (2nd edn, 1991)

Selected Poems, trans. by William Radice, London, Penguin, 1985

Selected Short Stories, trans. by Krishna Dutta and Mary Lago, London, Macmillan, 1991

Thompson, E. J., *Rabindranath Tagore: Poet and Dramatist*, Oxford University Press, 1926 (2nd edn, 1948)